Abortion Abolition

Abortion Abolition

Beyond Pro-Life vs. Pro-Choice Politics

Edited by
MAE ELISE CANNON

Andrea Smith, with contributions by
Andrew Cheung, Rob Dalrymple, and Soong-Chan Rah

CASCADE *Books* • Eugene, Oregon

ABORTION ABOLITION
Beyond Pro-Life Vs. Pro-Choice Politics

Copyright © 2025 Evangelicals4Justice. All rights reserved. Except for brief quotations in critical publications or reviews, no part of this book may be reproduced in any manner without prior written permission from the publisher. Write: Permissions, Wipf and Stock Publishers, 199 W. 8th Ave., Suite 3, Eugene, OR 97401.

Cascade Books
An Imprint of Wipf and Stock Publishers
199 W. 8th Ave., Suite 3
Eugene, OR 97401

www.wipfandstock.com

PAPERBACK ISBN: 979-8-3852-1202-6
HARDCOVER ISBN: 979-8-3852-1203-3
EBOOK ISBN: 979-8-3852-1204-0

Cataloguing-in-Publication data:

Names: Smith, Andrea, author. | Cannon, Mae Elise, editor.

Title: Abortion abolition : beyond pro-life vs. pro-choice politics / Andrea Smith ; edited by Mae Elise Cannon.

Description: Eugene, OR : Cascade Books, 2025 | Includes bibliographical references.

Identifiers: ISBN 979-8-3852-1202-6 (paperback) | ISBN 979-8-3852-1203-3 (hardcover) | ISBN 979-8-3852-1204-0 (ebook)

Subjects: LCSH: Pro-life movement—United States—History. | Abortion—United States—History.

Classification: HQ767.5.U5 .S65 2025 (print) | HQ767.5.U5 .S65 (ebook)

All Scripture quotations, unless otherwise indicated, are taken from the Holy Bible, New International Version®, NIV®. Copyright ©1973, 1978, 1984, 2011 by Biblica, Inc.™ Used by permission of Zondervan. All rights reserved worldwide. www.zondervan.com The "NIV" and "New International Version" are trademarks registered in the United States Patent and Trademark Office by Biblica, Inc.™

Contents

Biographies vii

Preface and Brief History—Rev. Dr. Mae Elise Cannon (Editor) xi

1. Eliminating a Faulty Paradigm   1
2. The Specter of Death within Pro-Life Politics   14
3. Why Pro-Choice Is Not Pro-Justice   37
4. Rethinking the Law   52
5. Abortion Abolition   65
6. Responses from Evangelicals4Justice Board Members   92
   Rev. Andrew Cheung
   Dr. Rob Dalrymple
   Rev. Dr. Soong-Chan Rah

Moving Forward   103

Bibliography   105

Biographies

REV. DR. MAE ELISE CANNON

REV. DR. MAE ELISE Cannon is the executive director of Churches for Middle East Peace (CMEP) and an ordained pastor in the Evangelical Covenant Church (ECC). Cannon formerly served as the senior director of Advocacy and Outreach for World Vision U.S. on Capitol Hill in Washington, DC; as a consultant to the Middle East for child advocacy issues for Compassion International in Jerusalem; as the executive pastor of Hillside Covenant Church located in Walnut Creek, California; and as director of development and transformation for extension ministries at Willow Creek Community Church in Barrington, Illinois. Cannon holds an MDiv from North Park Theological Seminary, an MBA from North Park University's School of Business and Nonprofit Management, and an MA in bioethics from Trinity International University. She received her first doctorate in American history with a minor in Middle Eastern studies at the University of California, Davis, focusing on the history of the American Protestant church in Israel and Palestine and her second doctorate in ministry in spiritual formation from Northern Theological Seminary. Her work has been highlighted in *The New York Times*, *The Washington Post*, CNN, *Chicago Tribune*, *Christianity Today*, *Leadership Magazine*, *The Christian Post*, *Jerusalem Post*, *EU Parliament Magazine*, *Huffington Post*, and other international media outlets.

BIOGRAPHIES

REV. ANDREW CHEUNG

Andrew Cheung is a self-professed "spiritual mutt" within Christian orthodoxy currently serving as the senior pastor at Washington Community Fellowship (wcfchurch.org), a multi-denominational church affiliated with the Mennonite tradition in Washington, DC. Bridging Western and Eastern influences, he delights in fostering the awareness of God's transformative work in our lives. Andrew also serves as a board member for Evangelicals4Justice (www.evangelicals4justice.org). In his downtime, he's most energized outdoors exploring the Washington, DC, region by bicycle and finding new places to rock-climb together with his family.

DR. ROB DALRYMPLE

Rob Dalrymple has been a professor, dean, and lead pastor for over thirty-four years at colleges, seminaries, and in the local church. He serves as the executive director of Determinetruth Ministries, a nonprofit parachurch organization focusing on teaching and equipping pastors and leaders worldwide. He hosts the Determinetruth podcast and writes a weekly blog on Patheos. His publications include: *Follow the Lamb: A Guide to Reading, Understanding, and Applying the Book of Revelation*; *Understanding the New Testament and the End Times: Why it Matters*; and newly released commentary on the Book of Revelation, *Revelation: a Love Story* (2024).

REV. DR. SOONG-CHAN RAH

Rev. Dr. Soong-Chan Rah is the Robert B. Munger Professor of Evangelism at Fuller Theological Seminary. Ordained in the Evangelical Covenant Church (ECC), Rah holds a ThD from Duke Divinity School, an MDiv and a DMin from Gordon-Conwell Theological Seminary, as well as a ThM from Harvard University. Rah has authored or coauthored over a half dozen, and many award-winning, books including *Unsettling Truths: The Ongoing,*

BIOGRAPHIES

Dehumanizing Legacy of the Doctrine of Discovery. He has spoken widely on the topics of the witness of the church, cross-cultural ministry, and social justice at academic conferences, seminaries, Christian colleges, local churches, denominational gatherings, and ministry conferences on both the domestic and global level.

ANDREA SMITH

Andrea Smith is a Christian activist and academic. She is the coordinator of Evangelicals4Justice. Her work has focused on racial justice, particularly anti-violence activism. She is the cofounder of INCITE! Women of Color Against Violence. She is the author of several books including *Conquest: Sexual Violence and American Indian Genocide*, which won the Gustavus Myers Outstanding Book Award (2005). She is the coeditor of *Evangelical Theologies of Liberation and Justice*. She served previously as a professor in the Ethnic Studies Department (Emerita) at the University of California, Riverside. In addition, she has a law degree from the University of California, Riverside.

Preface and Brief History

REV. DR. MAE ELISE CANNON

EVANGELICALS4JUSTICE (E4J) IS A community dedicated to providing a space for evangelicals to engage in constructive dialogue on justice-oriented issues. Many members of the E4J community, but not all, adhere to orthodox Christological beliefs about the person of Jesus but reject the commonly held assumption that evangelical theology is not liberative concerning issues of race, poverty, gender, sexuality, and other societal concerns. E4J members do not hold to monolithic theologies or ideologies, nor does this book attempt to universally represent any one singular view in terms of evangelical perspectives toward the question of the morality of abortion or the freedom of a woman to make choices over her own body. *However, this book does offer one collective call toward the trajectory of abortion abolition.* It does not represent the views of all E4J members but is offered in the spirit of dialogue in the hopes of offering a different possibility for conversation beyond the hardened divisions between those who define themselves as pro-life or pro-choice.

I am not this book's primary author, but I consider it a great privilege to help steward it coming into print. I wholeheartedly endorse and believe in the goal of minimizing the number of abortions by coming alongside people who hold various different beliefs. If we can agree to new strategies and goals that will both protect the rights of women to choose and also minimize the

Preface and Brief History

number of unwanted pregnancies, thus minimizing abortions—isn't that the best way forward? I hope this book might contribute toward such a future.

Taking a brief look at the history of abortion, the state of New York legalized abortion in 1970.[1] In 1973, based on the Fourteenth Amendment's "due process clause," the US Supreme Court decided the landmark case of *Roe v. Wade* and determined that it is a woman's choice whether or not to terminate her pregnancy. According to Planned Parenthood, *Roe v. Wade* "protected the right to abortion in all fifty 50 states, making abortion services safer and more accessible throughout the country."[2]

Before the 2024 presidential elections, the question of states' rights and federal abortion laws became front and center, and the country had never been more divided on the issue. The 2022 Supreme Court case of *Dobbs v. Jackson* overturned *Roe v. Wade* in a 6-to-3 ruling, a landmark decision that eliminated the right to abortion that had existed for almost fifty years.[3] Since then, numerous states have issued abortion bans or other restricted procedures. Some states considered the criminalization of abortion. The battle rages on as some states fight over access to abortions in the courtrooms, and other advocates work diligently to fight against restrictions and bans. On May 1, 2024, the *New York Times* tracked "Abortion Bans" across the country and identified twenty-one states that banned abortion or restricted the procedure earlier in pregnancy than the standard set by *Roe v. Wade*. Some states expanded and added legal protections by increasing access to abortion, serving as sanctuary states for women unable to obtain the procedure in their own districts or regions.

As of April 2024, fourteen states banned abortion at every stage of pregnancy, and most Republican states have some type of restrictions in effect. Abortion proved to be one of the most significant issues of the 2024 election season and was an issue on numerous state ballots, including Florida, Maryland, New York,

1. Kovach, "First Approval."
2. Planned Parenthood, "Historical Abortion Law," para. 12.
3. "*Dobbs v. Jackson* Decision."

and several others. Voters in seven states sided in favor of abortion rights, making the country significantly divided on how to address this critical issue that has a profound impact on women's bodies, the application of healthcare and medical treatment, and especially options made available to communities of color and economically disadvantaged women who may or may not be able to afford children.[4]

Since the 2022 Supreme Court decision and abortion bans and restrictions have started to go into effect, abortions have actually increased across the United States. According to a report by the Society of Family Plannings WeCount project, the year 2022 had 82,000 abortions per month, and 2023 had 86,000 per month. While the increase isn't huge, they attribute the rise to the availability of telehealth appointments where patients meet a physician online and then can have abortion medications mailed to them at home. As of May 2024, approximately 1 in 5 abortion appointments occured via telehealth.[5]

The February 2024 decision by the Alabama Supreme Court to uphold the decision that frozen embryos exist as "children" under the state's Wrongful Death of a Minor Act had significant implications on the criminalization of abortion. The Brookings Institute claims this was a "logical extension of the anti-abortion movement's long-time commitment to the notion of fetal personhood," acknowledging that many states have done so and applied personhood to the status of an embryo at any stage of development from fertilization to birth.[6] One of the results of this decision, according to Brookings, is that, de facto, women's bodies become the "scene of a crime." Uncertainty, confusing language, and unpredictability of when laws will be prosecuted all add to a situation of high stress, violations of privacy, and fear. In addition, the Brookings Institute expresses significant concern about how modern surveillance technologies enable law enforcement investigations of abortion crimes. Brookings challenges state legislatures, especially

4. Mulvihill and Kruesi, "Which States."
5. Simmons-Duffin and Nadworny, "6 Key Facts."
6. Dellinger and Pell, "Criminalization," para. 1.

those who claim there is no prosecutory intention, to ensure that "laws clearly and explicitly exempt women from prosecution."[7]

Our hope in this book, *Abortion Abolition*, is that human life will be valued, the termination of pregnancies will be minimized, a woman's right to choose will be the most protected, and all women, especially people of color, will not be criminalized. Andrea Smith writes the substance of this text with responses by board members from Evangelicals4Justice. Her main argument is against the criminalization of abortion and its disproportionate effect on women of color. We must abolish abortion because it is in the best interest of all—the lives of the unborn, the lives of mothers, and the lives of women of color who have been so disproportionately affected by the criminalization of abortion laws.

---

7. Dellinger and Pell, "Criminalization," para. 20.

CHAPTER 1

Eliminating a Faulty Paradigm

MANY EVANGELICALS HAVE A complicated relationship with abortion. Consider these two comments:

> "I don't want to vote for Trump, but I feel that if I don't, I'll be killing thousands of babies."

> "I asked all the Christians I know who are pro-life if they were to have an unwanted pregnancy, would they have an abortion. All the women said yes and all the men said no."

Author Shannon Dingle tells a heart-wrenching story in which her husband unexpectedly passed away. Days later, she realized she was probably pregnant and faced the possibility of a life-threatening pregnancy while caring for six children alone. She had been in the pro-life movement for many years and had been a speaker at pro-life conferences. But now, she saw no other option for herself than an abortion.[1]

Her story as well as the stories of those I quote above, indicate some of the tension evangelicals feel about the issue of abortion. Evangelicals generally present themselves as staunchly pro-life. This was not always the case. As Randall Balmer, Andrew R. Lewis,

---

1. Dingle, "I Was in the Pro-Life."

and many others have noted, evangelicals did not particularly mobilize against *Roe v. Wade*.[2]

In fact, the Southern Baptist Convention passed several resolutions in the early 1970s that were largely supportive of abortion in many circumstances. Most of the opposition to *Roe v. Wade* came from Roman Catholics. The evangelical shift toward pro-life politics is often attributed to the increased influence of the work of Francis Schaeffer, particularly his film *Whatever Happened to the Human Race?*, as well as to the political organizing by architects of the Religious Right to get evangelicals mobilizing in support of racial segregation to pick a more politically palatable banner around which to mobilize. As Robert P. Jones contends, despite the assumption that the banner issue of greatest concern to evangelicals is abortion, the 2020 election results were determined more by hostility to Black Lives Matter and antiracism politics than they were by opposition to abortion.[3] Things have perhaps not changed all that much.

Nevertheless, evangelicals are so identified with pro-life politics that this history is generally forgotten. In fact, being pro-life is so linked to evangelicalism that it is often not considered a political issue at all. And yet, what evangelicals espouse and what they actually practice are very different. Even those who are the most committed to pro-life politics can find themselves in difficult circumstances.

In addition, evangelicals often do not live by the sexual mores they espouse. Evangelicals themselves complain that abortion rates are high within Christian colleges.[4] *Christianity Today* writer Lauren Winner notes in her book *Real Sex* that three surveys of single Christians conducted in the 1990s found that two-thirds were not virgins.[5] In 1992, a *Christianity Today* survey of one thousand readers found that 40 percent had premarital sex, 14 percent had an affair, and 75 percent of those who had affairs did so when they

2. Balmer, *Bad Faith*.
3. Jones, "Race, Gender, and Christian Nationalism."
4. "Campus Life," 42–43.
5. Winner, *Real Sex*, 16.

were Christians.[6] In 2003, North Kentucky University found that 60 percent of students who signed sexual abstinence commitment cards broke their pledges.[7] And more recent statistics show that almost three-quarters of never-married eighteen-to-twenty-two-year-old evangelicals have engaged in some form of premarital sex. Among the fifteen-to-seventeen age group, evangelicals engaged in premarital sex at about the same rate as other religious groups.[8]

Lifeway Research found that 36 percent of women were attending church regularly at the time they had an abortion. And of all women who have had abortions, evangelical women are more likely to have more than one abortion. Most women say the church had no impact on their decision to have an abortion and believe that the church is not a safe place to let people know if they have an unwanted pregnancy. As a result, most report that no one in their church knows they had an abortion.[9]

In addition, many evangelicals, particularly during the 2020 presidential election, found it increasingly difficult to square their pro-life politics with the political options before them. John Piper, for instance, argued against the position that electing a corrupt political leader was an acceptable sacrifice to maintain pro-life policies.

> I think Roe is an evil decision. I think Planned Parenthood is a code name for baby-killing and (historically at least) ethnic cleansing. And I think it is baffling and presumptuous to assume that pro-abortion policies kill more people than a culture-saturating, pro-self pride.
>
> When a leader models self-absorbed, self-exalting boastfulness, he models the most deadly behavior in the world. He points his nation to destruction. Destruction of more kinds than we can imagine.

---

6. Robinson, "CT Readers Survey," 29–31.
7. Smith, *Native Americans*, 193.
8. Ayers, "Sexual Practices," 4.
9. Care Net, *Study of Women*.

Abortion Abolition

> It is naive to think that a man can be effectively pro-life and manifest consistently the character traits that lead to death—temporal and eternal.[10]

Others have said it is important to move beyond single-issue politics and essentially put this issue aside if the "pro-life" candidate's positions on other issues outweigh his or her position on abortion.[11] For instance, Rev. James Meeks stated:

> Evangelicals must be very careful not to be irrelevant.... Evangelicals will grab ... one issue—like abortion—and they think that because they take a tough stand on abortion then they have addressed a societal ill. I don't hear the same outcry from any evangelical pulpit about the unequal funding for education among the haves and the have-nots. I don't hear from the evangelical pulpit about the disparity in the prison population between blacks and whites, between the test scores of African American kids and white kids. If white kids couldn't read and black kids could ... the evangelical church would address it. If white kids were in jail and not going to college, the evangelical church would address it. So if you live in a society and you only address the things that face your ethnicity, you are not really concerned about social ills.[12]

Even more conservative evangelicals have rejected single-issue politics focusing on abortion. During the 2016 Republican primaries, Jerry Falwell Jr. endorsed Donald Trump, even though his pro-life qualifications were considerably weaker than those of other Republican candidates. His rationale: "All the social issues—traditional family values, abortion—are moot if ISIS blows up some of our cities or if the borders aren't fortified.... Rank-and-file evangelicals are smarter than many of the leaders. They are trying to save the country and may vote on the social issues next time."[13]

---

10. Piper, "Policies," paras. 24–26.
11. Harper, "We Go There."
12. Smith, *Native Americans*, 251.
13. Dean, "Just as I Am," 38.

Some have adopted a "consistent pro-life ethic," which is described by the Consistent Life Network as follows: "We are committed to the protection of life, which is threatened in today's world by war, abortion, poverty, racism, the death penalty, and euthanasia. We believe these issues are linked to a 'consistent ethic of life.' We challenge those working on all or some of these issues to maintain a cooperative spirit of peace, reconciliation, and respect in protecting the unprotected."[14] Shane Claiborne has stated: "We need to be pro-life from the womb to the tomb. Abortion and euthanasia, the death penalty and war, poverty and health care—all of these are issues of life and death. And they are issues Jesus cares about because they affect real people."[15]

This shift in the pro-life paradigm to a more consistent life framework was evidenced in the 2017 Evangelicals for Life conference organized by the Ethics and Religious Liberty Commission of the Southern Baptist Convention. While abortion was certainly discussed at this conference, other pro-life issues, such as racial justice, immigration reform, and disability, were given equal time. There was as much criticism of President Trump's Muslim ban as there was of pro-choice politics. Eugene Cho expanded on pro-life politics to center issues of racism, religious intolerance, and xenophobia during his keynote address. He stated that if we are pro-life, we must be concerned about not only American lives but also Syrian lives. We must be concerned about not only Christian lives but also Muslim lives. And if we are pro-life, we must unapologetically state that Black lives matter.

Meanwhile, some evangelicals are concerned that a pro-life position does not allow for proper consideration of the lives of women who might be seeking abortions. They have argued for essentially a pro-choice perspective on abortion that holds that abortion should be safe, available, and rare.

Charles Camosy, in his thoughtful *Beyond the Abortion Wars*, notes that the pro-life versus pro-choice binary does not do justice to the complex positions most people have. "Most Americans are

---

14. Consistent Life Network, "Mission Statement," para. 2.
15. Claiborne and Campolo, *Red Letter Revolution*, 85.

'pro-choice' in some situations, and most are 'pro-life' in some situations."[16] He cites a Public Religion Research Institute survey from 2011 that found that "seven in ten Americans say the term 'pro-choice' describes them somewhat or very well, and nearly two-thirds simultaneously say the term 'pro-life' describes them somewhat or very well. This overlapping identity is present in virtually every demographic group."[17]

While these complicated engagements may require different assumptions, they all assume that the pro-life versus pro-choice paradigm is correct but needs to be expanded, complicated, set aside when necessary, or applied more consistently. I wish to argue that the problem is the pro-life versus pro-choice paradigm itself. I am not arguing that evangelicals should renounce pro-life commitments to become pro-choice. Rather, the problem is the framework for understanding the issues and the possible solutions to the issues. Whenever we struggle with a paradigm, especially one that creates dilemmas for people, it is always worth asking whether there is another way to view the issue that may lead to other possibilities. In fact, as I will argue in greater detail in chapters 2 and 3, both the pro-life and pro-choice positions are actually more similar than they are different, in that they both fundamentally promote racial, economic, and disability disparity, and neither position is capable of promoting life or choice in our communities.

Instead, I argue that we should adopt an abortion abolition framework. Abolition is often understood as ending a practice or institution. However, to quote Ruth Wilson Gilmore, "Abolition is not *absence*, it is *presence*. . . . So those who feel in their gut deep anxiety that abolition means knock it all down, scorch the earth and start something new, let that go. Abolition is building the future from the present, in all of the ways we can."[18] It is the creation of new systems and relationships that renders a practice or institution unnecessary. I argue that an abolition framework permits us to engage people across the current pro-life versus

---

16. Camosy, *Abortion Wars*, 12.
17. Jones, Cox, and Laser, "Committed to Availability," para. 4.
18. Gilmore, "Making Abolition," para. 2.

pro-choice divide and more effectively addresses the root causes of why there is abortion. I explore what an abortion abolition framework offers in greater detail in chapter 5.

WHY I LEFT THE PRO-LIFE AND PRO-CHOICE MOVEMENTS

When I first accepted Christ into my life as a teenager, I was already pro-life. I was also a young feminist, and because I was introduced to evangelical feminist work even before I became a Christian, I identified as an evangelical feminist from the beginning of my faith journey. Consequently, I was also involved in feminist organizing throughout my life as a Christian. However, I found myself always at odds with non-Christian feminists over the issue of abortion and argued that there should be a space in the feminist movement for those who are pro-life.

However, I became increasingly alienated from the pro-life movement because I did not see much regard in it for the lives of women who found themselves seeking an abortion. It seemed that the pro-life movement was completely dehumanizing women who had to make difficult choices, and calling them baby killers at abortion clinics did not feel particularly Christlike to me. I also had friends who became pregnant unexpectedly, went to pregnancy crisis centers, and were traumatized by the experience. They reported that the people in the centers did not care at all about them but were only trying to pressure them into a decision without providing any resources to address the reasons they felt compelled to have an abortion. One friend, in particular, said, ironically, that it was only her engagement with the pro-choice community that enabled her to have a child because there she found people willing to let her process her choices, help her problem-solve, and think through all the possibilities before her.

I am not suggesting that my experiences with pregnancy crisis centers and the pro-life movement are true for everyone. Undoubtedly, many women have received strong, unconditional support. Nonetheless, I was shaped by my experience, which led me to leave the pro-life movement.

While I still believed (and continue to believe) that an unborn child is indeed a life, I switched my involvement from the pro-life movement to the pro-choice movement because I initially felt that the latter was honoring the lives of women and the difficult choices they have to make rather than being set on promoting abortion per se. However, after about six years in that movement, I became alienated from pro-choice politics as well.

My biggest problem with the pro-choice movement, as I witnessed it, was that while it claimed to support choice for women, it was actually concerned about choice for only some women, namely white, middle- or upper-class women. Women of color and the poor, by contrast, had too many babies and needed to be stopped from procreating by any means necessary. This became quickly apparent in the early 1990s with the marketing of long-acting hormonal contraceptives with dubious safety records, like Depo-Provera and Norplant. I was working at a feminist health center when a young black woman came in asking about contraceptives. The white health worker immediately suggested that she go on Norplant. However, a trainee, a woman of color, asked if she was a smoker. When the client said yes, the trainee said that smoking was a contraindication for Norplant; that is, women who smoke should probably use a different contraceptive. The trainee was reprimanded, not for giving incorrect information, but because the supervisor thought this client needed to be on long-acting contraceptives, regardless of the impact on her health. I have no doubt that if the client had been white and middle class, the supervisor would have informed her of all the contraindications of Norplant. Meanwhile, at another prominent organization, I found that hotline workers were told never to tell callers about the possible side effects of Norplant and Depo-Provera. I was scheduled to appear on television with the head of that organization to address why it provided Norplant only in African American communities, but the organization canceled, saying it was not prepared to defend its practices.

Meanwhile, I ended up on the board of an affiliate of another prominent pro-choice organization. Because the board was dominated by women of color, it was often at odds with the white-dominated national office. In particular, we decided to do an informed-consent campaign in our city on Norplant and Depo-Provera. We did not tell women to use or not use it but did provide full information on the possible side effects of these contraceptives. We found that many women of color became interested in this work, even if they did not define themselves as "pro-choice." But the national office sent us orders to cease and desist from doing work on informed consent. At another prominent pro-choice organization, the leaders were supporting anti-immigration legislation because they said immigrants were "overpopulating the United States." Basically, what I found was that when it came to reproductive rights, the mainstream movement supported "choice" for white, middle-class women but population control for everyone else.

Again, not everyone will have these sorts of experiences in the pro-choice community. Many organizations adopt a framework of reproductive justice that addresses racial and economic disparity and has a more holistic analysis.[19] Even within mainstream organizations, there are many persons who work tirelessly to fight for more inclusive frameworks. Nonetheless, I personally found that the mainstream movement occasionally engaged in critique in a tokenistic way but did not primarily concern itself with the most marginalized women in the pro-choice movement.

These contradictions became evident when I asked women whether they defined themselves as pro-life or pro-choice.

Example 1

Me: Are you pro-choice or pro-life?

Respondent 1: Oh, I am definitely pro-life.

Me: So, you think abortion should be illegal?

Respondent 1: No, definitely not. People should be able to have an abortion if they want.

---

19. See, for instance, SisterSong: https://www.sistersong.net/.

Me: Do you think then that there should not be federal funding for abortion services?

Respondent 1: No, there should be funding available so that anyone can afford to have one.

Me: But you would call yourself pro-life?

Respondent 1: Yes, I am very pro-life.

Example 2

Me: Would you say you are pro-choice or pro-life?

Respondent 2: Well, I would say that I am pro-choice, but the most important thing to me is promoting life in Native communities.

Example 3

Me: Would you say you are pro-choice or pro-life?

Respondent 3: The fetus is a life. But sometimes, that life must be ended.

There is a presumed intractable divide between those who consider themselves pro-life and those who are pro-choice. In actuality, however, people's actual positions on abortion are often much messier. These responses make it difficult to place the women neatly into "pro-life" or "pro-choice" camps. Is Respondent 1 pro-life because she says she is pro-life? Or is she pro-choice because she supports the decriminalization of and public funding for abortion? Is Respondent 2 pro-choice because she says she is, or is she pro-life because she says promoting life is her priority? And what do we make of Respondent 3?

I started to see that people cannot easily be categorized as either pro-life or pro-choice—they have complicated positions. And also, it doesn't make sense to declare myself completely loyal to everything the pro-life or pro-choice movement does; it makes sense to recognize that both movements do messed-up things. The solution is to eliminate this paradigm altogether and analyze things in their full complexity. The paradigm frequently forced me into allying with organizations regardless of whether the policy or practice they espoused was racist, classist, or otherwise problematic. It forced me to treat people in the other camp as "the enemy" rather than see the possibilities of working together if the issues were framed differently. And ultimately, I saw that the most marginalized communities remained marginalized in both movements.

The evolution of the pro-life and pro-choice movements reflects the contradictions I experienced in both movements. In the next section, I will explore how these contradictions have been addressed as well as what remains unaddressed within these movements. I would suggest that the problem is that they substitute the strategy for the long-range vision. That is, the goal of the pro-life movement is to criminalize abortion. The goal of the pro-choice movement is to decriminalize it. However, if we change our goal to promoting healthy, vibrant communities in which all lives are valued, we become open to discussing which strategies (including criminalizing or decriminalizing abortion) will be most effective in achieving this goal. But because the mainstream movements have made the strategy the goal itself, they have often found themselves supporting positions that would, in the end, seem contradictory. Furthermore, the pro-life and pro-choice frameworks are fundamentally similar in that they are both based on racist and economically exploitative operating assumptions that, in the end, promote neither life for unborn children nor choice for women.

This book is not focused on espousing a particular political position regarding electoral politics. Rather, it seeks to interrogate some of the political assumptions that give rise to people feeling trapped inside various political dilemmas. In interrogating these assumptions, I hope to create more political and theological space that might enable us to develop a more effective way to promote the lives of unborn children, their mothers, and their communities. In the end, for people who remain committed to either the criminalization or decriminalization of abortion, I hope that an abortion abolition framework will provide more opportunities for people across that strategic divide to work together on other strategies for the benefit of all. In addition, such a framework provides more room for creative possibilities and dialogue to think of how we, as Christians, can create a world in which the conditions that give rise to women feeling they need to seek an abortion would be fundamentally transformed.

ABORTION ABOLITION METHODOLOGIES

This book draws from thinkers across the political and theological spectrum. No matter where one is on that spectrum, one has a tendency to disregard arguments if they come from the "wrong" camp. The Southern Baptist Convention's recent condemnation of critical race theory, despite the number of evangelicals who are also critical race theorists, exemplifies this tendency. But I have also experienced this same tendency in less conservative circles. For instance, I applied for a job in a gender studies department once but was informed that my Christianity disqualified me because I was a "right-wing religious nut."

However, an abolition methodology calls for a different approach. It recognizes that the world we want to create is a world for which we yet have no words. Consequently, no one has all the answers, and everyone in the world has at least part of the answer. The fact that we might disagree with 90 percent of what a person says should not stop us from hearing the other 10 percent.

Matthew 25:35–40 states:

> "For I was hungry and you gave me something to eat, I was thirsty and you gave me something to drink, I was a stranger and you invited me in, I needed clothes and you clothed me, I was sick and you looked after me, I was in prison and you came to visit me."
>
> Then the righteous will answer him, "Lord, when did we see you hungry and feed you, or thirsty and give you something to drink? When did we see you a stranger and invite you in, or needing clothes and clothe you? When did we see you sick or in prison and go to visit you?"
>
> The King will reply, "Truly I tell you, whatever you did for one of the least of these brothers and sisters of mine, you did for me."

Eliminating a Faulty Paradigm

We generally focus on the importance of Christians attending to those in need. But this verse also tells us Jesus may appear in unexpected places in the guise of unexpected people. We never know where and from whom we may receive an insight from God. "For now we see through a glass, darkly; but then face to face: now I know in part; but then shall I know even as also I am known" (1 Cor 13:12 KJV). Remaining open to the unexpected increases our chances of gaining new insights into bringing the world in closer conformity to God's kingdom. In his exchange with the Canaanite woman in Matthew 15:21–28, Jesus models for us how to receive insight from all people while remaining clear about God's world. She challenges him, and he accepts the challenge. We, too, can be challenged by others without losing our faith. Unfortunately, we often approach challenges through fear rather than with openness. But true faith is not grounded in fear and remains open to where Jesus might be sharing a word with us. In that spirit, I offer wisdom I have learned from diverse sources, not to convince people that I have the "right" answer but to open more space for collective thinking on how we can go forward in creating a better world for all.

CHAPTER 2

The Specter of Death within Pro-Life Politics

THE PRO-LIFE POSITION MAINTAINS that the fetus is an unborn child, a life; hence, abortion should be criminalized. Consequently, the pro-life position situates its argument around moral claims regarding the sanctity of life. In a published debate on pro-life versus pro-choice positions on abortion, Gary Crum (former vice president of South Carolina Citizens for Life) argued that the pro-life position is "ethically pure."[1] Because of the moral weight he grants to the protection of the life of the fetus, Crum contends that abortion must be criminalized. Any immoral actions that impact others should be a "serious crime under the law."[2] The pro-choice position counters this argument by asserting that the unborn child is a fetus and not a life, and hence, the policy must be directed toward protecting a woman's ability to control her own body. To quote sociologist Thelma McCormack's response to Crum: "Life truly begins in the . . . hospital room, not in the womb."[3] Gloria Feldt, former president of Planned Parenthood, similarly asserts

---

1. Crum and McCormack, *Abortion*, 54.
2. Crum and McCormack, *Abortion*, 28.
3. Crum and McCormack, *Abortion*, 121.

that if the fetus is established as a life, the principles of *Roe v. Wade* must necessarily be discarded.[4]

I disagree with both of these perspectives. I believe that the fundamental issue of concern in the pro-life position is not whether or not the fetus is an unborn child and, hence, a human life, but the conclusion it draws from this assertion—that because the fetus is a life, abortion should be criminalized. Generally, it is often assumed that the best way to deal with a bad thing is to make it a crime. Not making a bad action a crime is seen as somehow supporting that action. This assumption must be fundamentally challenged because it fails to consider the negative consequences of criminalization.

Furthermore, many ways exist to address bad things in our society without relying on criminalization. By not questioning criminalization as its primary strategy, the pro-life position inadvertently promotes death. Many evangelicals have actively organized to reform the criminal justice system. Their insights can inform our understanding of the problems related to criminalizing abortion.

EVANGELICALS FOR CRIMINAL JUSTICE REFORM

Recently, there has been increased mobilization across the political and theological spectrum for criminal justice reform. This mobilization has questioned the assumption that the best way to deal with crime is through increased incarceration. Studies show that not only do prisons not solve social problems, such as crime, but they are also more likely to increase rather than decrease crime rates.[5] Most people in prison are there for drug- or poverty-related crimes. Prisons do not provide treatment for drug addiction, and it is often easier to access drugs in prison than on the street. For people in prison because of poverty-related crimes, a prison record guarantees a much harder time securing employment once

---

4. Feldt, *War on Choice*, 90.
5. Currie, *Crime*.

they are released. And incarcerating people for not following the norms of society pushes them further out of that society into a violent context where they will be even less likely to follow social norms. Consistently, study after study indicates that prisons do not decrease crime rates.[6]

Charles Colson was a prophetic voice among evangelical Christians who pointed out in the 1970s that increased incarceration was not the best way forward in reducing crime rates.[7] Formerly an attorney with the Nixon administration, Colson served time in prison for his role in the Watergate break-in. Colson recounts in his autobiography, *Life Sentence*, the vow he made to his fellow prisoners upon his release: "I'll never forget this stinking place or you guys."[8] True to his word, Colson immediately became involved in prison reform and ministry, culminating in the formation of Prison Fellowship. Prison Fellowship started with a staff of six but now has a budget of over $42 million and over 260,000 volunteers worldwide.[9] His decades-long work in prison advocacy led Colson to conclude:

> The whole system of punishment today is geared toward taking away people's dignity, putting them in an institution, and locking them up in a cage. Prisons are overcrowded, understaffed, dirty places. Eighty percent of American prisons are barbaric—not just brutal, but barbaric. . . . Prison as a punishment is a failure.
>
> Mandatory sentences and longer sentences are counterproductive . . . the tougher the laws, I'm convinced, the more lawless and violent we will become. As for public safety, it can hardly be said that prisons contribute to public safety. . . . Prisons obviously are not deterring criminal conduct. The evidence is overwhelming that the more people we put in prison, the more crime we

---

6. Box and Hale, "Economic Crisis," 139.
7. Smith, *Native Americans*.
8. Colson, *Life Sentence*, 24.
9. Prison Fellowship International, *Portraits*.

have. All prisons do is warehouse human beings and at exorbitant cost.[10]

Prison Fellowship does not argue that criminalization or prisons should be eliminated. But it calls for an approach based on restorative justice (compared to "retributive justice"), which involves restoring both those who commit harm and the victims of that harm to society rather than simply punishing the former. Prisons, while sometimes viewed as necessary for the small minority of "hardened criminals," are generally at odds with the principles of restorative justice for most people who have been criminalized. In *Life Sentence*, Colson does not simply critique "inhumane" prisons; rather, he characterizes prisons as inherently inhumane. The inhumanity of prisons then means that prisoners who are not dangerous offenders are more likely to come out dangerous. "The more people we put in prison, the more crime we have."[11] Numerous studies have demonstrated that more prisons and more police do not lead to lower crime rates.[12] Colson echoed the findings of this research when he declared: "I'm absolutely convinced that the principal cause of crime in America is the prison system itself."[13] Prison Fellowship asserts: "Research has shown little correlation between crime rates and the number of people housed in a state's

---

10. Colson, "Prison," 27.

11. Colson, *Justice*, 130.

12. Currie, *Crime and Punishment*; Donziger, *Real War on Crime*, 42 and 162; Walker, *Sense and Nonsense*, 130.

The Rand Corporation found that California's three strikes legislation, which requires life sentences for three-time convicted felons, did not reduce the rate of "murders, rapes, and robberies that many people believe to be the law's principal targets" (Walker, *Sense and Nonsense*, 130). In fact, changes in crime rate often have more to do with fluctuations in employment rates than with increased police surveillance or increased incarceration rates (Box and Hale, "Economic Crisis"; Colvin, "Controlling the Surplus"; Jankovic, "Labour Market.") Concludes Steven Walker, "Because no clear link between incarceration and crime rates, and because gross incapacitation locks up many low-rate offenders at a great dollar cost to society, we conclude as follows: gross incapacitation is not an effective policy for reducing serious crime" (Walker, *Sense and Nonsense*, 130).

13. Colson, "Prison Reform," 51.

prison."[14] Daniel Van Ness, former director of Justice Fellowship, cites a 1986 Rand Corporation study that found that offenders who were given prison sentences actually committed crimes more quickly upon release and more often than similar offenders who were put on probation.[15] He argues that as many as 80 percent of all people in prison should not be there.[16] At the 1999 Justice Fellowship Forum on Restorative Justice, Van Ness similarly deconstructed the "fear of crime," noting that fear of crime is highest in communities with the lowest crime rates.[17] Prison Fellowship notes that the ten states with the largest prison population reductions from 2008 to 2016 also saw crime reduced by an average of more than 15 percent.[18] As Prison Fellowship notes, the exponential growth in prisons was not in response to growing crime rates.[19]

Similarly, in his seminal text *Rethinking Incarceration*, Dominique Gilliard, director of Racial Righteousness and Reconciliation for the Evangelical Covenant Church, analyzes the crisis of mass incarceration in the United States: the nation contains only 5 percent of the world's population but accounts for 25 percent of the world's incarceration. It has more jails and prisons than it does colleges and universities. In some areas of the country, there are more people living behind bars than on college campuses. One out of every twenty-five people sentenced to death is falsely convicted. Thirteen states have no minimum age for prosecuting children as adults, with children as young as eight being sentenced as adults. Eighty thousand inmates per day are locked in solitary confinement, which Gilliard argues should be seen as a form of torture.[20]

The Bible is the foundation for evangelicals espousing criminal justice reform. Van Ness argues that the form of punishment favored by the Bible is restitution. Biblical principles of punishment

14. Justice Fellowship, "1997 Criminal Justice."
15. Van Ness, "Restoring Crime's Victims."
16. Colson, "Sentenced for Life," 52; Colson, "God Behind Bars," 32.
17. Harvey, "Christians and Crime."
18. DeRoche et al., *Outrageous Justice*, 34.
19. DeRoche et al., *Outrageous Justice*, 34.
20. Gilliard, *Rethinking Incarceration*, 26.

as applied to contemporary society dictate that drug offenders should go into treatment centers run on Christian principles, and those arrested for other offenses should be involved in restitution and community-sentencing programs—programs that do not remove offenders from the community but instead allow them to remain free while they make restitution to their victims. Colson takes a similar Bible-based position to denounce prisons: "Prison is a relatively new invention, really only about 200 years old as a purpose of punishment. You'll find throughout the Bible that prisons are there for political reasons or for people awaiting trial, but not for punishment. Biblically, we are told to make restitution. . . . I believe in alternatives to incarceration for nonviolent offenders."[21]

Gilliard has further argued that evangelicals must de-carcerate their theologies: "People are declaring that they are not content with living in a carceral state, and they are building a movement that has the potential to birth something novel, restorative, and transformative. We serve a God who desires liberation, reconciliation, and reintegration for those behind bars. God invites the church to participate in setting the captives free."[22] He calls on Christians to adopt a different framework altogether based on the themes of restoration, transformation, and redemption.

There has been much debate among Christians about prison reform. For instance, some argue for reforming policies within prisons, while others argue that such reforms simply strengthen the presumption that prisons are the primary solution for addressing social harm. However, it seems one area where people can agree is that critical to reducing the negative impacts of the prison-industrial complex on society is to reduce the number of people in prison. This can happen through three strategies: (1) change the outcome of what happens when someone receives a conviction (that is, change the relationship between "crime" and "punishment"); (2) challenge overcriminalization (this requires us to challenge what is considered a "crime" in the first place); and (3) change the conditions that give rise to people committing

21. Colson, "Prison," 14.
22. Gilliard, *Rethinking Incarceration*, 199.

crimes in the first place (that is, go beyond intervening after harm has occurred and create conditions that reduce harm in the first place—the implication of this will be discussed in greater detail in chapter 5). In the next section, I will focus on strategy to address overcriminalization and its implications for abortion policies.

THE PROBLEM WITH CRIMINALIZATION

Prison Fellowship has noted that one of the reasons for the exponential growth in prisons is overcriminalization. So many actions have become crimes that one can even commit a crime without knowing it.

> The Bible emphasizes the importance of criminal intent in dealing with guilty individuals. These values have continued in our own culture for centuries. Indeed, criminal intent is the line differentiating a crime from an innocent mistake. This fundamental principle, however, is being eroded by Congress in a misguided attempt to protect people and property. As a result, Americans are in danger of a criminal justice system that criminalizes commonplace, innocent behaviors. Through the vast number of federal criminal laws and regulations, and the lack of criminal intent requirements in many of those laws, the federal government is criminalizing activities undertaken with no reasonable intent to harm anyone. For example, a person could face federal criminal charges and time in federal prison for abandoning a snowmobile in a life-threatening blizzard, digging up arrowheads, or even violating another country's laws by packing frozen lobsters in plastic bags instead of paper.[23]

Prison Fellowship tells the story of a man who followed standard procedure by diverting a pipe to the sewer during a crisis in a nursing home. Unbeknownst to the nursing home, the sewer pipe led to the Potomac River, and he received a criminal record

---

23. DeRoche et al., *Outrageous Justice*, 46.

for following his employer's policy.[24] In a case like this, nothing is served by incarcerating such an individual. Education is needed for nursing home personnel to know where their sewer pipes are connected.

There might be other actions deemed less "innocent" that are not effectively addressed by criminalization. One such might be drug addiction. No one argues that drug addiction is a good thing. However, drug addiction is a disease that the individual cannot easily control, and hence, criminalization does not effectively address it. By contrast, if we were to address addiction as a health issue rather than a criminal justice issue, we could invest our resources into treatment facilities that can more effectively address the problem.

Another example of the ineffectiveness of criminalization is criminalizing those who are houseless. Many laws are passed to essentially criminalize being homeless, everything from sitting outside to sleeping in one's car. While many of these laws have been found unconstitutional, many police officers will arrest someone who is houseless anyway. Then, when the person fails to make a court appearance, largely because the person is houseless, he or she is subject to arrest for that, even though the underlying arrest would have been thrown out. The irony is that the state ends up spending more money incarcerating a person who is houseless than if it simply provided housing for that person. One myth is that the houseless suffer from an underlying condition, such as mental illness, that makes them prone to being houseless, and that issue needs to be addressed first. But the major problem is actually the lack of housing itself. Houselessness creates trauma that could be solved if people just had homes. Thus, rather than addressing houselessness through criminalization, we could spend much less money addressing it by providing affordable housing.[25]

---

24. DeRoche et al., *Outrageous Justice*, 33.

25. National Law Center on Homelessness and Poverty, "Housing Not Handcuffs," for more information on the problems with criminalizing homelessness.

In addition, criminalization strategies often backfire. An example is criminalization as the primary strategy for addressing domestic violence. Domestic violence activists formed their strategy around the slogan that sexual and domestic violence "is a crime"[26] and thus pushed for increased criminalization of sexual/domestic violence through mandatory arrest policies, no-drop prosecution policies, longer sentencing, etc. This approach, sadly, did not reduce domestic violence rates but often furthered women's victimization. For instance, as a result of the strengthened anti-domestic-violence legislation, battered women kill their abusive partners less frequently, but batterers do *not* kill their partners less frequently.[27] With mandatory arrest laws, police officers frequently arrest those being battered rather than the batterers. A study of mandatory arrest laws in Wisconsin found that they *increased* mortality rates among Black domestic violence survivors by 98 percent (and white survivors by 9 percent), for an overall increase in mortality of 64 percent.[28] Ironically, laws passed to protect battered women are actually protecting their batterers! Is this to suggest that domestic violence is acceptable? Of course not. Rather, it suggests that there could be multiple ways to address domestic violence. For instance, one of the primary reasons violence survivors go back home to batterers is that they lack affordable housing. Perhaps focusing on providing affordable housing would keep more survivors safe and decrease their mortality rates.

Challenging criminalization is not to sanction the practice itself. Those who critique the overreliance on criminalization to address domestic violence, for instance, are certainly not pro–domestic violence. Rather, they ask whether criminalization is the best strategy to address this issue, given its negative consequences. Similarly, it is important to look at the effects of criminalizing abortion to determine if that strategy is beneficial overall. If we determine that the consequences of criminalization make that strategy not beneficial, it does not mean we do not care about abortion.

26. Richie, *Arrested Justice,* for more analysis.
27. Butterfield, "Study Shows."
28. Sherman and Harris, "Increased Death Rates," 1–20.

Rather, it may open up the possibility of thinking of other strategies that might be more effective with fewer unintended consequences.

In the case of abortion, many negative consequences come with criminalization that should make us rethink our reliance on it as the primary strategy for reducing abortion rates.

Criminalizing Abortion Contributes to the Buildup of the Prison-Industrial Complex

As Mimi Kim notes in her analysis of what she calls the "carceral creep," focusing on criminalization as the solution for social problems contributes to the buildup of the prison-industrial complex, even if the number of people incarcerated for a particular social problem is relatively small. She notes that at the same time the anti-violence movement began to invest in criminalization as the primary solution to domestic and sexual violence, the prison system began to skyrocket. Now, the majority of people in prison are not there for domestic and sexual violence cases, but cumulatively, the investment in carcerality contributes to prison growth.[29]

As an example, the Violence Against Women Act was attached to the punitive Violent Crime Control and Law Enforcement Act, which increased the use of the death penalty, added over fifty federal offenses (many of which criminalized youth of color), eliminated Pell Grants for prisoners, and expanded the prison-industrial complex by $9.7 billion. Anti-violence advocates heralded it as "feminist" legislation but failed to critique its problematic components, which hurt many domestic violence survivors. Furthermore, these anticrime measures make abused women more likely to find themselves in prison if partners coerce them to engage in illegal activity. When men of color are disproportionately incarcerated because of these laws, the entire community, particularly women, who are often the community caretakers, is negatively impacted.

---

29. Kim, "Carceral Creep."

When we divert all our energies into criminal justice solutions for social justice problems like abortion, we divert all our resources to the prison system, which then becomes a self-perpetuating industry, hence the term "prison-industrial complex." As Mae Elise Cannon notes in *Beyond Hashtag Activism*, prisons have become the go-to solution for social problems like inadequate educational systems, failed mental health systems, and uncompassionate immigration systems. By relying on criminal justice solutions, we do not put energy into creating sustainable and life-giving educational, mental health, and immigration policies.[30] Similarly, when we focus on criminalization as the only strategy by which to reduce abortion rates, we pay insufficient attention to creating sustainable communities in which abortion would no longer seem to be necessary for many people.

Criminalizing Abortion Disproportionately Impacts Communities of Color

Criminalization, in general, disproportionately impacts communities of color, poor communities, and other marginalized communities. As Dominique Gilliard and Mae Elise Cannon have argued, churches must look at how their investment in criminalization has contributed to the criminalization of blackness. States Gilliard: "The church must reckon with the reality that ever since black people were stolen from Africa and trafficked to this land, they have been dehumanized, abused, criminalized, incarcerated, exploited for profit, and governed in distinctively sinister ways. . . . Given the racism, dehumanization, and economic exploitation of our criminal justice system, the church must refuse to remain silent. . . . Christians must join the freedom caravan and take part in the ongoing work of reimagining true justice."[31]

---

30. Cannon, *Beyond Hashtag Activism*.

31. Gilliard, *Rethinking Incarceration*, 44. For further information: Cannon, *Social Justice Handbook*.

Prison Fellowship has similarly affirmed that criminal justice reform is integrally involved with ending institutional racism in society at large.

> For more than 40 years, our experience in prisons has brought us face to face with racism, an individual and systemic sin that violates human dignity and worth. We have witnessed firsthand the stark racial disparities in the criminal justice system. Racial bias and injustice contribute directly to these trends, as do other pervasive upstream issues like instability in housing and family structures, unequal access to quality education, and poverty.
>
> Due to the complexity of the justice system, the law provides limited but important opportunities to correct racial disparity. Prison Fellowship works hard every day to advance justice that restores and reflects the God-given value of all persons. In some cases, legislation can help mitigate inequalities, and we have been advocating for proportional sentencing and justice that addresses the systemic biases and prejudices borne by people of color. We also acknowledge that the ultimate elimination of racial bias requires each of us to consider our own beliefs, attitudes, and positions in light of the Gospel and with the help of the Holy Spirit. . . .
>
> As U.S. history bears witness with the abolitionist and Civil Rights movements, the Church is uniquely equipped to contribute Gospel-focused, nonviolent protest and advocacy for racial reconciliation and communal healing.[32]

The history of the buildup of the prison-industrial complex cannot be separated from the racial history of the United States. The racial background of the prison population before the Civil War was white. After the Civil War, the Thirteenth Amendment was passed, which prohibits slavery—except for prisoners. The slavery system was then essentially replaced by the convict-leasing system, which was often even more brutal. Under slavery, slave owners at least had a financial incentive to keep slaves alive. In the

---

32. Prison Fellowship, "Statement."

convict-leasing system, no such incentive existed—if a prisoner died, she or he could simply be replaced by another prisoner.[33] The regime of the prison was originally designed to "reform" the prisoner by creating conditions for penitence (hence the term "penitentiary").[34] After the Civil War, however, prisons adopted the similar regimes of punishment found in the slavery system, which coincided with the re-enslavement of Black communities into the convict-leasing system.[35] The American Bar Association reports that today, although Black people make up 13.4 percent of the population, they make up 22 percent of fatal police shootings, 47 percent of wrongful conviction exonerations, and 35 percent of death penalty executions. African Americans are incarcerated in state prisons at five times the rate of white people.[36] One-third of all Native and Black students with a disability are suspended or expelled despite the legal protections of these students against suspensions and expulsions.[37] Native people are the people most likely to be killed by police violence and are incarcerated thirty-eight times more than the national average.[38] Black, Latinx, and Native peoples are disproportionately arrested and convicted for drug offenses beyond their actual drug use.[39] By contributing to the buildup of the prison system, the criminalization of abortion contributes to increased racism and social marginalization of oppressed communities.[40] As will be discussed in the next section, specifically, women of color and poor women are impacted by the criminalization of abortion.

Many evangelicals have correctly pointed to the inherent racism undergirding the pro-choice movement (which I will discuss

33. Davis, *Are Prisons Obsolete?*; Mancini, *One Dies.*
34. Ignatieff, *Just Measure of Pain.*
35. Davis, *Are Prisons Obsolete?*
36. Inman, "Racial Disparities."
37. Losen et al., "Suspended Education in California."
38. Millet, "Native Lives Matter, Too."
39. Camplain et al., "Racial/Ethnic Differences."
40. Alexander, *New Jim Crow,* for more on racism in the criminal justice system.

in greater detail in the next chapter). They argue that the promotion of abortion and contraceptives by pro-choice organizations often stems from a eugenics-based population-control ideology in which it is presumed that the birthrates of communities of color must be controlled. "One other factor undergirding the eugenics-population control matrix is racism. As minorities have become more vocal . . . the racist element of the population control movement remains. . . . For example, there is evidence that the opening of state-supported birth control clinics is closely related to the concentrations of poor black people in various states. . . . At this juncture, population control . . . and racism become one and the same—planned death for those unfortunate souls unable to resist."[41]

If we take this critique seriously, then we must also apply it to the pro-life movement and its investment in the prison-industrial complex, which is an institution of population control for communities of color in the United States. When we rely on a strategy that is inherently racialized, then we must rethink that strategy.

Criminalizing Abortion Increases Numbers of Unsafe Abortions Without Reducing Abortion Rates in a Racially and Economically Disproportionate Manner

There is much debate about the extent to which criminalizing abortion impacts abortion rates or deaths from abortion. Many studies have found that countries that have criminalized abortion have the same rates of abortion as do countries that have legalized it. The only difference is that countries that have abortion restrictions have more unintended pregnancies.[42] One study indicates that decriminalizing abortion can actually *decrease* abortion rates. In fact, studies have suggested that criminalizing abortion

41. Whitehead, "Death Control," 11.

42. Guttmacher Institute, "Unintended Pregnancy." See also MacKinnon, "What Actually Happens"; Vogelstein and Turkington, "Abortion Law"; Boseley, "Criminalising Abortion"; Rosenthal, "Legal or Not"; Panetta, "States Passing."

only increases maternal mortality and severe health complications without decreasing abortion rates. These studies have found that while there is often a general increase in reported abortions after abortion decriminalization because abortions are underreported when they are criminalized, abortion rates generally decrease once they are no longer underreported. The reason is not necessarily that decriminalizing abortion directly decreases abortion rates. Rather, when abortion is criminalized, there is no post-abortion counseling geared toward preventing unwanted pregnancies in the future because abortion providers are financially motivated. When abortion is integrated into the health system, then women have more access to contraceptive counseling, particularly after an abortion. Since 40 percent of abortions are repeat abortions, decriminalizing abortion dramatically decreases repeat abortions.[43]

In addition, there has been much debate about whether or not criminalizing abortion increases death rates from abortion. Glenn Kessler notes that the death rate from abortions was relatively low right before *Roe v. Wade*, and pro-choice proponents frequently exaggerate the number of abortion-related deaths in the immediate years before *Roe v. Wade*.[44] But, as the Guttmacher Institute contends, that was because those who were relatively well-to-do were able to access abortion legally before *Roe* in seventeen states or could otherwise skirt the law by having physicians with whom they had a personal relationship perform the abortion, or they were able to travel long distances to have one. Nonetheless, women of color and poor women who had less access to these options were disproportionately impacted by the restrictive abortion laws and unsafe abortions.[45]

Even if we accept the Guttmacher Institute's reasons for the low death rate from abortion right before *Roe v. Wade*, it means the law itself did not protect people against deaths from abortions; it was the ability of people to avoid the law that provided protection.

---

43. Faundes and Shah, "Evidence Supporting." See also Broom, "Abortion Rates."

44. Kessler, "Planned Parenthood's False."

45. Gold, *Lessons from Before Roe*.

In countries where there is less ability to avoid the law, restrictive abortion laws increase maternal mortality without decreasing abortion rates. And even in the United States, states with the most restrictive abortion laws have the highest infant and maternal mortality rates.[46] In addition, women of color and poor women are disproportionately impacted by restrictive abortion laws. Thus, these laws are racially and economically discriminatory.

Some may argue that the increased death rates for women might be worth it to save the lives of unborn children. This rationale is flawed for several reasons. First, these laws do not actually decrease abortion rates. So, overall, they lead to more deaths for children and mothers. Second, why engage in a strategy that pits the lives of mothers against those of children? Why not look for policies and practices that can save the lives of both? The reason we do not is because we are conditioned to think that the only way to address a social problem is through criminalization, and we do not look for other solutions. Third, we should always be disturbed by any solutions that have racially and economically disproportionate impacts.

Criminalizing Abortion Contributes to the Criminalization of Miscarriages and Stillborn Births, Particularly for Women of Color and Poor Women

Laws that are used to criminalize abortion are also often used to criminalize miscarriages or stillborn births. One study notes that anti-abortion statutes are often used to arrest women who have miscarriages or stillborn births under the idea that they did something to cause a child's death.[47] For instance, Keysheonna Reed was arrested for having miscarried twins and later disposing of their bodies. Katherine Dellis was similarly convicted until pardoned. In both cases, it was determined that neither had done anything to kill their children—they had died of miscarriages. But they were still

---

46. Panetta, "States Passing."
47. Paltrow and Flavin, "Arrests."

convicted of improperly treating a "corpse." Imagine the trauma of losing one's children only to be incarcerated! Consider the case of Marshae Jones, who may soon face a grand jury in Alabama. The police say that when Ms. Jones was five months pregnant, she started a fight that led to her being shot in the stomach and losing her fetus. "That child is dependent on its mother to try to keep it from harm, and she shouldn't seek out unnecessary physical altercations," explained Lt. Danny Reid of the Pleasant Grove, Alabama, police force. So, even though she was the victim of a gunshot and lost a child that she wanted, she was the one deemed culpable rather than the person who shot her. Jamie Fisher went to the hospital because she was in pain. Instead of treating her, the hospital had her arrested when it found she had drugs in her possession. She then died in jail from the ectopic pregnancy the hospital refused to treat.

Criminalization thus has unintended consequences for women—again, particularly for poor women and women of color—who are not even seeking abortions. When women have to fear being arrested for a miscarriage, they can be deterred from seeking health care if their pregnancies are endangered. Criminalization can thus promote death rather than life.

The response of the pro-choice movement to such laws is to deny the personhood of the fetus. I do not think that is the problem. Rather, it is the assumption that all actions that negatively impact the personhood of the unborn child must be criminalized. When women fear criminalization, they are more likely to engage in risky behaviors that endanger their lives and the lives of their unborn children.

Criminalizing Abortion Increases Vulnerability for Women with Addictions

Abortion laws are used to criminalize women who are pregnant and have addictions. The premise underlying criminal laws that punish drug-using pregnant women is that unborn children may be viewed as separate legal entities with rights hostile to and in conflict with those of the pregnant woman. While no one would argue that addictions are a good thing, we must question whether criminalization is the best way to assist a pregnant woman who has an addiction. First, addictions are not a choice and are not easily ended. Second, there is often a lack of treatment facilities for pregnant women. Third, criminalizing addiction makes it more likely a woman with an addiction will not seek health care, thus actually further endangering her own life and the life of her child. Finally, criminalization disproportionately impacts women of color and poor women, who are less likely to have private doctors and thus more likely to be subject to criminalization through the public health system.

Consider this illustration: In 1997, the South Carolina Supreme Court held that viable unborn children are persons under state law. Further, a pregnant woman with an addiction could be prosecuted for child abuse. The South Carolina attorney general's office said the state could prosecute such a woman with murder that could result in the death penalty for her as well as her physician. As a result, (1) infant mortality in the state increased for the first time in a decade; (2) the state saw a 20 percent increase in abandoned babies; (3) the number of women seeking treatment for drug addiction declined dramatically.[48]

Moreover, for some women, an unwanted abortion may be the only way to avoid arrest and imprisonment for continuing a pregnancy to term despite a drug problem. For instance, Martha Greywind, a pregnant woman with an addiction, was criminally charged with endangering her child while pregnant. To avoid going to prison, she was forced to have an abortion she did not want.[49] Sadly, a "pro-life" law contributed to an abortion.

As Dorothy Roberts and others have noted, women of color are more likely to be arrested for drug use because the high rates of poverty in communities of color make it more likely they come in contact with government agencies where their drug use can be detected. While white pregnant women are slightly *more* likely to

48. National Advocates for Pregnant Women, "What's Wrong?"
49. Paltrow and Flavin, "Arrests."

engage in substance abuse than Black women, public health facilities and private doctors are more likely to report Black women than white women to criminal justice authorities.[50] Meanwhile, pregnant women who would like treatment for their addiction can seldom get it because treatment centers do not meet the needs of pregnant women. One study found that two-thirds of drug treatment centers do not treat pregnant women.[51] Furthermore, the criminalization approach is more likely to drive pregnant women who are substance abusers from seeking prenatal or other forms of health care for fear of being reported to the authorities.[52]

Unfortunately, even communities of color—those that identify as both pro-life and pro-choice—have supported the criminalization of women of color who have addiction issues because they focus on what they perceive to be the moral culpability of women of color for not protecting the life of their children. But to question criminalization as a strategy to protect unborn children is not to say they do not need protection. Rather, if criminalization makes it more difficult for women with addictions to seek help, then we are actually putting more children in danger. Instead, we could focus on increasing access for pregnant women to treatment. Furthermore, addiction is itself a result of social and political conditions, such as racism and poverty; churches need to alleviate these conditions rather than target women who they victimize. Criminalization provides no resources for pregnant women to end their addictions; it simply penalizes them for continuing a pregnancy. It is imperative that churches address the problem rather than the symptom of the problem with respect to addictions to truly promote life in our communities.

---

50. Maher, "Criminalizing Pregnancy," 115–35; Roberts, *Killing the Black Body*, 175.

51. Roberts, *Killing the Black Body*, 189.

52. Roberts, *Killing the Black Body*, 190.

PRO-CHOICE AND CRIMINALIZATION

As I have argued throughout this chapter, what is currently distinguishing the pro-life movement is less a commitment to life and more a commitment to criminalization, which actually promotes death, particularly in poor communities and communities of color. But the pro-choice movement has not challenged the criminalization paradigm either. In the next chapter, I will discuss the problems with the pro-choice movement in greater detail. But in terms of criminalization specifically, many pro-choice organizations have supported financial incentives for poor women with addictions to accept sterilizations and have either supported or at least not challenged laws that would sentence women with addictions to sterilizations or long-acting hormonal contraceptives.[53] Part of this political inconsistency is inherent in the articulation of the "pro-choice" position. But another reason is that many in the pro-choice camp have also not questioned criminalization as the appropriate response to reproductive health concerns. They may differ as to which acts should be criminalized, but they do not necessarily question the criminalization regime itself.

CONCLUSION

The major flaw in the pro-life position is not its claim that the unborn child is a life but its assumption that because the unborn child is a life, abortion should be criminalized. A commitment to criminalization of social issues necessarily contributes to the growth of the prison system because it reinforces the notion that prisons are appropriate institutions for addressing social problems rather than causes of the problems itself. Given the disproportionate impact of criminalization on communities of color, support for criminalization as public policy also implicitly supports racism.

---

53. I also found, in my years of organizing, that many pro-choice organizations would offer financial incentives for women to be sterilized or take long-acting hormonal contraceptives with dubious safety records.

Many pro-life organizations have rightfully been ardent opponents of population-control programs and policies—advocating against the promotion of dangerous contraceptives or the promotion of sterilization in third-world countries. But the support of criminalization supports a system that promotes population control for communities of color, that is, the prison-industrial complex. To promote life, we have to think of other strategies for reducing abortion rates that do not promote death as their unintended consequence.

Perceiving abortion to be the taking of a life does not require criminal justice punishment as a necessary response. Criminalization individualizes solutions to problems resulting from larger economic, social, and political conditions. Consequently, it is inherently incapable of solving social problems like abortion or addressing "crime." Alternative social formations and institutions can address these large-scale political and economic conditions and are the appropriate place to address social issues, such as abortion. Churches could be ideally suited to address these conditions in a manner that actually promotes life.

There is no evidence to suggest that involving the criminal justice system will reduce the number of abortions, given that it has not been effective in reducing crime rates or addressing social problems, generally speaking. And countries that do criminalize abortions do not see decreased abortion rates; they see increased infant and maternal mortality rates. In addition, increased criminalization disproportionately impacts people of color. An interrogation of the assumptions behind the pro-life movement (as well as the pro-choice response to it) suggests that what distinguishes the pro-life position is not so much its explicit commitment to life (since criminalization promotes death rather than life, particularly in communities of color and poor communities) as its implicit commitment to criminal justice interventions in reproductive justice issues.

Russell Moore of the Southern Baptist Convention said, in an address to the 2017 Ethics and Religious Liberty Commission Evangelicals for Life conference, that the practice of abortion is often based on a logic of disposability. He argued that Jesus primarily concerned himself not with those in power but with those who are socially marginalized. To be pro-life is to be anti-disposability. Similarly, those who work on prison reform note that criminalization is also based on a logic of disposability. Rather than address the root causes of crime (such as racism, social marginalization, economic disparity, lack of access to mental health services, lack of access to drug treatment, etc.), criminalization disposes of the person who represents those root causes. As a result, when we focus on disposing of the symptoms of social, political, and economic inequality, we never actually develop strategies to effectively end inequality. To illustrate, when schools have a high suspension/expulsion rate for those deemed problem students, that is an independent factor that decreases overall school performance for the remaining students. If a student is not functioning well in a school system, that indicates that the educational model of that school may need to be changed. But instead of changing the educational model so that it handles the diverse needs of students, some schools simply expel those students who are not effectively served by it. As a result, the education remains substandard for the students who remain.[54]

This critique of criminalization as the solution for social problems has been prevalent within evangelical circles for at least sixty years, championed by organizations like Prison Fellowship. If many evangelicals are clear on the inability of criminalization to solve most social problems, is it such a huge leap to question why criminalization could solve the problem of abortion? As stated in a *World* magazine article: "The mother of the aborted child [is] a person who needs compassion, not incarceration."[55]

Some evangelicals have argued that with respect to electoral politics, they are firmly committed to pro-life policies, but they are not single-issue voters. My contention is that even a single-issue voter with respect to abortion should not equate the desire to end abortion with a commitment to criminalization. Rather, it

54. Losen et al., "Suspended Education in California."
55. Olasky, "Pro-Life Priorities," 34.

is important for us to think of strategies that promote life while simultaneously reducing social harm. I address some possibilities in chapter 5.

CHAPTER 3

Why Pro-Choice Is Not Pro-Justice

IN THE PREVIOUS CHAPTER, I argued that the pro-life framework is less about a commitment to life and more about a commitment to criminalization, which actually promotes death. In this chapter, I deconstruct the pro-choice framework as that which supports justice, particularly for women. That is, pro-choice advocates generally argue that pro-life proponents do not care about the lives of women and are willing to sacrifice them for the lives of their unborn children. I argue that the pro-choice framework actually forsakes justice for women and reflects an abandonment of social justice principles.

CHOICE VERSUS JUSTICE/RIGHTS

A variety of scholars and activists have critiqued the choice paradigm because it rests on essentially individualist, consumerist notions of "free" choice that do not take into consideration all the social, economic, and political conditions that frame the so-called choices women are forced to make.[1] Rickie Solinger contends that in the 1960s and 1970s, abortion rights advocates initially used the term "rights" rather than "choice"—rights, understood as those benefits owed to all humans regardless of access

---

1. Patchesky, *Abortion and Women's Choice*; Smith, *Conquest*; Solinger, *Beggars and Choosers*.

to special resources. By contrast, argues Solinger, the concept of "choice" is connected to the possession of resources, thus creating a hierarchy among women who are capable of making legitimate choices.[2] Consequently, since under a capitalist system, those with resources are granted more choices, it is not, therefore, inconsistent to withdraw reproductive rights choices from poor women and Indigenous women through legislation such as the Hyde Amendment (which restricts federal funding for abortion) or to restrict the number of children that women on public assistance can have.[3] Her argument can be demonstrated from the writings of Planned Parenthood itself. In 1960, it commissioned a study that concluded that poor and working-class families lack the rationality to do family planning, and this lack of "rationality and early family planning as middle-class couples" are "embodied in the particular personalities, world views, and ways of life" of the poor themselves.[4] As Solinger states: "'Choice' also became a symbol of middle-class women's arrival as independent consumers. Middle-class women could afford to choose. They had earned the right to choose motherhood if they liked. According to many Americans, however, when choice was associated with poor women, it became a symbol of illegitimacy. Poor women had not earned the right to choose."[5]

What her analysis suggests is that, ironically, while the pro-choice camp contends that the pro-life position diminishes the rights of women in favor of "fetal" rights, the pro-choice position does not ascribe inherent rights to women either. Rather, women are ascribed reproductive choices if they can afford them or if they are deemed legitimate choice-makers.

---

2. Solinger, *Beggars and Choosers*, 6.

3. See Mink, *Whose Welfare?*, for further analysis of how welfare reform marks poor women and women of color as women who make "bad choices" and hence should have these choices restricted through marriage promotion, family caps (or cuts in payments if recipients have additional children), and incentives to use long-acting hormonal contraceptives.

4. Rainwater, *And the Poor Get Children*, 5, 167.

5. Solinger, *Beggars and Choosers*, 199–200.

WHY PRO-CHOICE IS NOT PRO-JUSTICE

William Saletan's history of the evolution of the pro-choice paradigm illustrates the extent to which this paradigm is not actually supportive of the interests of women. He contends that pro-choice strategists, generally affiliated with the then-named National Abortion Rights Action League (NARAL), intentionally rejected a rights-based framework in favor of one focused on privacy from "big government." That is, the government should not have the right to intervene in women's right to decide if they want to have children. This approach appealed to those with libertarian sensibilities who otherwise might not sympathize with feminist causes. This strategy enabled the pro-choice side to keep *Roe v. Wade* intact—but only in the most narrow of senses. It also undermined any attempt to achieve a broader justice agenda actually centered on the rights of all women (not just white, well-to-do women) because the strategy behind this approach could be used against a broader agenda. For instance, pro-life advocates could use the same argument against federal funding for abortions through the Hyde Amendment because the government had no business providing funding for abortion services.[6] Consequently, Saletan argues that the pro-choice movement succeeded precisely because it decentered social justice issues and the rights of women.[7]

IMPACT OF CHOICE POLITICS ON MARGINALIZED COMMUNITIES

From the pro-life perspective, one may wonder, what would be an argument against the Hyde Amendment? The issue with the Hyde Amendment is that it introduces an economically and racially discriminatory framework for those who have access to abortion services. American Indian women, for instance, largely access services through the Indian Health Services, which is federally funded. As a result, they are denied access to abortion services essentially on the basis of race. Whatever policy a country has should not be discriminatory.

6. Saletan, *Bearing Right*.
7. Saletan, "Electoral Politics and Abortion."

Furthermore, restrictions on abortions can become another strategy to coerce Native women or economically marginalized women into sterilization procedures or into taking long-acting hormonal contraceptives of dubious safety records in order to avoid the trauma of unwanted pregnancy. The strategy of coupling restrictive abortion with sterilization policies is evident in the proposed 1993 North Carolina General Assembly HB 1430, which stated: "The Department of Human Resources shall ensure that all women who receive an abortion funded through the State Abortion Fund receive Norplant implantation and do not remove it unless the procedure is medically contraindicated."[8] This legislation sought to pressure women into accepting long-acting hormonal contraceptives during a vulnerable period when they were facing an unwanted pregnancy.

Similarly, in the Northwest Territories of Canada, the Status of Women Council uncovered punitive abortion policies at the Stanton Hospital in Yellowknife, which services Inuit women. Women were denied anesthesia during abortion services as punishment for seeking abortions. One woman was told by her doctor: "This really hurt, didn't it? But let that be a lesson before you get yourself in this situation again."[9] This controversy was uncovered when a rape victim, Ellen Hamilton, told the media her abortion had been worse than the rape: she was given no counseling, pinned down, and given no anesthesia during the procedure. One woman who went in for an abortion and a tubal ligation on the same day reported that she was told, "The anesthesiologist does not believe in abortions; we will administer the anesthetic following the abortion, for the tubal ligations." Increasing the pain and trauma associated with abortion or making it inaccessible puts even more pressure on Native women to agree to sterilizations or dangerous contraceptives. Given the long history of sterilizations against Native women without their informed consent, offering

---

8. State Congress of North Carolina, "House Bill 1430."
9. Walsh, "Abortion Horror Stories," A-5.

free sterilization to Native women while denying abortion services can have a genocidal impact on Native communities.[10]

From a pro-life perspective, of course, the reasonable response to this problem might be, rather than expand abortion services to American Indian women, to restrict them for everyone else. But from the pro-choice perspective, there is no good excuse for pro-choice organizations not to zealously advocate against the Hyde Amendment unless they believe some women, on the basis of race, should have less access to the rights they claim are essential. Yet, pro-choice organizations often develop strategies that marginalize women of color and poor women. Planned Parenthood and NARAL both supported the Freedom of Choice Act in the early 1990s, which retained the Hyde Amendment.[11] One of NARAL's petitions stated: "The Freedom of Choice Act (FOCA) will secure the original vision of *Roe v. Wade*, giving *all* women reproductive freedom and securing that right for future generations."[12] This rhetoric leaves the impression that poor women and indigenous women do not qualify as "women." Again, the pro-choice movement is as susceptible to adopting racially and economically discriminatory policies as is the pro-life movement. Whatever the policy on abortion is, it should apply equally to all women. Building on this analysis, I would argue that while there is certainly a sustained critique of the "choice" paradigm, particularly among women-of-color reproductive rights groups,[13] the choice paradigm continues to govern much of the policy of mainstream groups in a manner that marginalizes Indigenous women and women of color, poor women, and women with disabilities.

One example is the extent to which pro-choice advocates narrow their advocacy of legislation to the choice of whether to have an abortion without addressing the conditions that give rise to a woman having to make this decision in the first place.

10. Smith, *Conquest*, for a longer discussion on this topic.
11. Saletan, *Bearing Right*.
12. Smith, "Beyond Pro-Choice." Emphasis added.
13. Silliman et al., *Undivided Rights*; Ross and Roberts, *Radical Reproductive Justice*; Nelson, *Women of Color*.

Consequently, politicians, such as former president Bill Clinton, are heralded as "pro-choice" as long as they do not support legislative restrictions on abortion, regardless of their stance on other issues that may equally impact the reproductive choices women make. Clinton's approval of federal welfare reform that placed poor women in the position of possibly being forced to have an abortion because of cuts in social services, for instance, while often critiqued, is not critiqued as an "anti-choice" position.

Advocates of the "choice" paradigm often take positions that negatively impact marginalized communities. For instance, this paradigm often makes it difficult to develop nuanced positions on the use of abortion when the unborn child is determined to have abnormalities. Focusing solely on the woman's choice to have or not have the child overlooks the larger context of a society that sees children with disabilities as having lives not worth living and provides inadequate resources to women who may otherwise want to have them. As Martha Saxton notes: "Our society profoundly limits the 'choice' to love and care for a baby with a disability."[14] Furthermore, as many disability justice advocates have noted, our society generally sees people with disabilities as "better dead than disabled."[15] As Charles Camosy points out, 90 percent of unborn children who are diagnosed with Down syndrome are aborted.[16] If our response to disability is simply to facilitate the process of aborting children who may have disabilities, we never actually focus on changing the economics and policies that make raising children with disabilities difficult. A justice-centered analysis would focus on ending ableism (the ideology that only people who are able-bodied are valued) and supporting disability justice rather than promoting the disposability of victims of ableism.

14. Saxton, "Disability Rights," 374–93.
15. Coleman, "Face to Face."
16. Camosy, *Beyond the Abortion Wars*, 36.

Why Pro-Choice Is Not Pro-Justice

PRO-CHOICE AND POPULATION-CONTROL POLITICS

Pro-choice groups often have a difficult time maintaining a critical perspective on dangerous or potentially dangerous contraceptives that are often disproportionately promoted in poor communities, communities of color, and the Global South; they argue that women should have the "choice" of contraceptives. Many scholars and activists have documented the dubious safety record of Norplant and Depo-Provera, two long-acting hormonal contraceptives.[17] In fact, lawsuits against Norplant have forced an end to its distribution (although Norplant is still on the shelves and can be given to women). In 1978, the Federal Drug Administration (FDA) denied approval for Depo-Provera as contraception on the grounds that (1) dog studies confirmed an elevated rate of breast cancer, (2) there appeared to be an increased risk of birth defects in human fetuses exposed to the drug, and (3) there was no pressing need shown for use of the drug as a contraceptive.[18] In 1987, the FDA changed its regulations and began to require cancer testing in rats and mice instead of dogs and monkeys; Depo did not cause XYZ cancer in these animals, but major concerns regarding its safety persist.[19]

Also problematic is the manner in which contraceptives are promoted in communities of color, often without informed consent.[20] Yet none of the mainstream pro-choice organizations

---

17. Krust and Assetoyer, *Study of the Use*; Masterson and Gutherie, "Taking the Shot"; Roberts, *Killing the Black Body*; Smith, "Better Dead Than Pregnant."

18. Masterson and Gutherie, "Taking the Shot."

19. Jordan, "Toxicology."

20. Krust and Assetoyer, *Study of the Use*; Masterson and Gutherie, "Taking the Shot"; Smith, "Better Dead Than Pregnant." I was a co-organizer of a reproductive rights conference in Chicago in 1992. Their hotline workers from the Chicago chapter of a national pro-choice organization reported that they were told to tell women seeking contraception that Norplant had no side effects. In 2000, women in a class I was teaching in California told the class hotline workers from this same pro-choice organization were not allowed to tell callers of the side effects of Depo-Provera because they were supposed to promote the contraceptive. Of course, these problems around informed consent are not

have ever seriously taken on the issue of informed consent in their agendas. Indeed, Gloria Feldt, former president of Planned Parenthood, equated opposition to Norplant and Depo-Provera to opposition to "choice" in her book *The War on Choice*.[21] Planned Parenthood and NARAL actually opposed restrictions against sterilization abuse, despite the thousands of women of color who were being sterilized without their consent, because such policies would interfere with women's "right to choose."[22] Particularly disturbing was the support given by these organizations to the Center for Research on Population and Security, headed by Stephen Mumford and Elton Kessel, which distributes globally a form of sterilization, quinacrine, that has no proven safety record, is highly vulnerable to abuse, and was being promoted by the Center from an explicitly anti-immigrant perspective.[23] It was so unsafe it was later banned for contraceptive use in India.

---

necessarily a national policy from this organization or uniform across all their agencies.

21. Feldt, *War on Choice*, 34, 37.

22. Nelson, *Women of Color*, 144; Patchesky, *Abortion and Women's Choice*, 8.

23. Quinacrine is a drug used to treat malaria. It is inserted into the uterus, where it dissolves, causing the fallopian tubes to scar, rendering the woman irreversibly sterile. Family Health International conducted four in vitro studies and found quinacrine to be mutagenic in three of them. It, as well as the World Health Organization, recommended against further trials for female sterilization, and no regulatory body supports quinacrine. However, the North Carolina–based Center for Research on Population and Security circumvented these bodies through private funding from such organizations as the Turner Foundation and Leland Fikes organization (which incidentally funds pro-choice *and* anti-immigrant groups). It has been distributing it for free to researchers and government health agencies. There are field trials in eleven countries, with more than seventy thousand women sterilized. In Vietnam, a hundred female rubber plant workers were given routine pelvic exams during which the doctor inserted the quinacrine without their consent. So far, the side effects linked with quinacrine include ectopic pregnancy, puncturing of the uterus during insertion, pelvic inflammatory disease, and severe abdominal pains. Other possible concerns include heart and liver damage and exacerbation of preexisting viral conditions. In one of the trials in Vietnam, a large number of cases were excluded from the data because of serious side effects. "Controversy over Sterilization Pellet"; Norsigian, "Quinacrine Update."

Despite the threat to reproductive justice that this organization represents, a prominent mainstream feminist organization featured it at their 1996 Feminist Expo because, the organizers informed me, it promoted "choice" for women. Then, in 1999, Planned Parenthood almost agreed to sponsor a quinacrine trial in the United States until outside pressure forced them to change their position.[24] A prevalent ideology within the mainstream pro-choice movement asserts that women should have the "choice" to use whatever contraception they want. Such positions do not consider (1) that a choice among dangerous contraceptives is not much of a choice; (2) that the pharmaceutical companies and the medical industry have millions of dollars to promote certain contraceptives while advocacy groups have few resources to provide alternative information on these same contraceptives; and (3) that dire social, political, and economic conditions of women make dangerous contraceptives the best of bad options. A similar critique of choice, made in *Christianity Today*, links the choice framework to consumerism (in this case, contraceptive consumerism): "Transpose the political notions of liberty into a commercial framework and you get choice, with the maximization of choice as a supreme value."[25]

One reason that such groups have not taken a position on informed consent on potentially dangerous contraceptives is their investment in population control. As Betsy Hartmann has argued, while contraceptives are often articulated as an issue of "choice" for white women in the first world, they are articulated as an instrument of population control for women of color and women in the Global South.[26] The historical origins of Planned Parenthood are inextricably tied to the eugenics movement. Its founder, Margaret Sanger, increasingly collaborated with eugenics organizations during her career and framed the need for birth control in terms of the

---

24. Committee on Women, Population and the Environment, internal correspondence, 1999; Saheli Collective, *Quinacrine;* Freedman, "Two Americans."

25. "Fear Not the Disabled."

26. Hartmann, *Reproductive Rights and Wrongs.*

need to reduce the number of those in the "lower classes."[27] In a study commissioned in 1960, Planned Parenthood concluded that poor people "have too many children,"[28] and something must be done to stop this trend to "disarm the population bomb."[29]

I will not rehearse the problematic analysis of this population paradigm, which essentially blames third-world women for poverty, war, environmental damage, and social unrest while ignoring the root causes of all these phenomena (including population growth)—colonialism, corporate policies, militarism, and economic disparities between poor and rich countries.[30] However, as Hartmann documents, the United Nations Population Fund has long been involved in coercive contraceptive policies throughout the world. The Population Council, which is an NGO that conducts research on health and development, produced Norplant and assisted in Norplant trials in Bangladesh and other countries, which were done without the informed consent of the trial participants.[31] In fact, trial administrators often refused to remove Norplant when requested.[32] All these population organizations intersect to promote generally long-acting hormonal contraceptives of dubious safety around the world.[33] While population-control advocates are increasingly more sophisticated in their rhetoric and often talk about ensuring social, political, and economic opportunity, they still focus on reducing population rather than providing social, political, and economic opportunity.

---

27. Roberts, *Killing the Black Body*, 73.

28. Rainwater, *And the Poor Get Children*, 2.

29. Rainwater, *And the Poor Get Children*, 178.

30. Bandarage, *Women*; Hartmann, *Reproductive Rights and Wrongs*; Silliman and King, *Dangerous Intersections*. For an extended discussion, see Smith, *Conquest*.

31. Hartmann, *Reproductive Rights and Wrongs*.

32. Cadbury, *Human Laboratory*.

33. Hartmann, *Reproductive Rights and Wrongs*.

REPRODUCTIVE JUSTICE AND PRO-CHOICE POLITICS

It is important to note that many primarily women-of-color-led reproductive justice organizations have argued for a much more justice-centered reproductive justice agenda.[34] However, this organizing still often takes place within the pro-choice paradigm, which negatively impacts the actual ability to develop a broader justice-centered agenda. As an example, many women-of-color groups mobilized to attend the 2004 March for Women's Lives in Washington, DC, to expand the focus of the march from a narrow pro-choice abortion rights agenda to a broad-based reproductive rights agenda. While this broader agenda was reflected in the march, it became co-opted by the pro-choice paradigm in the media coverage of the march. My survey of the major newspaper coverage of the march indicates that virtually no newspaper described the march as anything other than a pro-choice, abortion rights march.[35]

Another unfortunate consequence of uncritically adopting the "choice" paradigm is the tendency of reproductive rights advocates to analyze simplistically who their political friends and enemies are in the area of reproductive rights. That is, all who call themselves pro-choice are political allies, while all who call themselves pro-life are political enemies. An example of this rhetoric is Gloria Feldt's description of anyone who is pro-life as a "right-wing

---

34. See, for instance, Silliman et al., *Undivided Rights*; Ross and Roberts, *Radical Reproductive Justice*; Nelson, *Women of Color*.

35. Newspapers that focused solely on abortion rights include the *New York Times, Bridgeport Connecticut Post, New York Newsday, Syracuse Post-Standard, Bergen County (NJ) Record, Baltimore Sun, Memphis Commercial Appeal, Richmond (VA) Times Dispatch, Marin (CA) Independent Journal, Salt Lake Tribune, Madison (WI) Capital Times, Dayton Daily News, Milwaukee Journal Sentinel, Cleveland Plain Dealer, Minneapolis Star Tribune, Chicago Daily Herald, Chicago Sun-Times, Columbus (OH) Dispatch,* and *San Francisco Chronicle*. A few papers covered other issues, including health-care access, AIDS prevention, birth control, women's rights around the world, and various other political causes.

extremist."³⁶ This sort of simplistic analysis does not do justice to the complex political positions people inhabit. As a result, we often lose opportunities to work with people with whom we have sharp disagreements but who may shift their positions with different political framings and organizing strategies.

To illustrate, Planned Parenthood is often championed as an organization that supports a woman's right to choose. Yet, as discussed previously, its roots are in the eugenics movement, and today it is heavily invested in the population-control establishment. It continues to support population-control policies in the third world; it almost supported the development of quinacrine in the United States; and it opposed strengthening sterilization regulations that would protect women of color.

Meanwhile, the North Baton Rouge Women's Help Center in Louisiana is a crisis pregnancy center that articulates its pro-life position from an antiracist perspective. It argues that Planned Parenthood has advocated population control, particularly in communities of color. It critiques the Black Church Initiative for the Religious Coalition for Reproductive Choice for contending that charges of racism against Margaret Sanger are "scare tactics."³⁷ It also attempts to provide its services from a holistic perspective—it provides educational and vocational training, general equivalency diploma (GED) classes, literacy programs, primary healthcare and pregnancy services, and child placement services. Its position is, "We cannot encourage women to have babies and then continue their dependency on the system. We can't leave them without the resources to care for their children and then say, 'Praise the Lord, we saved a baby.'"³⁸

Now, if one is articulating a pro-choice position from the perspective of women who are most particularly marginalized, it would seem that both groups support some positions that are beneficial and some positions that are detrimental. So, if pro-choice organizations are committed to supporting the lives of women,

36. Feldt, *War on Choice*, 5.
37. Blunt, "Unflappable Condi Rice," 22.
38. Blunt, "Unflappable Condi Rice," 23.

why should they necessarily work with Planned Parenthood and reject the Women's Help Center? The problem with the pro-choice movement is that its only concern about the well-being of a woman is the moment at which she decides to have an abortion. Consequently, the pro-choice framework is not, in the end, actually pro-women, particularly not pro-women of color or poor women.

BEYOND DISPOSABILITY: MOURNING EVERY DEATH

As I mentioned previously, the pro-choice movement bases its argument solely on the foundation that the fetus is not a life. This contributes to rendering children who are aborted based on disability, gender, or other discriminatory means as disposable. It provides no foundation by which women who miscarry can mourn the loss of their child. If a pregnant woman miscarries because she is assaulted, it offers her no means by which this harm can be redressed.

These untenable positions can be addressed by challenging the assumption that one cannot support the decriminalization of abortion while also mourning every death that comes from an abortion. If we shift from a perspective that assumes "no harm has happened" to one of "attempting to reduce the harm," we can establish policies that do not require us to harden our hearts to the pain women feel when they lose an unborn child (whether by miscarriage or abortion). We can hold the lives of women and unborn children together as we strive to create a world in which all lives can be honored and respected. As Charles Camosy notes, many people who define themselves as pro-choice actually do see the fetus as an unborn child, but "they don't think the law can protect the fetus without seriously threatening the rights of the mother."[39] He goes on to argue that many people do not think abortion is a big deal at all and that the decision to have an abortion is not

---

39. Camosy, *Beyond the Abortion Wars*, 11.

"heart-wrenching" but akin to a decision about coloring one's hair.[40] This may be true, but the pro-life versus pro-choice paradigm itself elicits this response. That is, if the paradigm revolves around whether the fetus/unborn child is a life, then those concerned about the autonomy of women are almost compelled to devalue the lives of unborn children to affect their public policy preferences. However, if the discussion is decentered from whether the fetus/unborn child is a human life to what strategies are more effective and least harmful in promoting the lives of unborn children and women, then it becomes more morally possible to value life while disagreeing with the criminalization of abortion.

Similarly, as many evangelicals espousing a consistent life politic have argued, those espousing pro-life politics would be more compelling to society at large if they also mourned the deaths of all people (say, for instance, those on death row), not just unborn children. This would include not reducing women who seek abortions to the category of "baby-killers" but recognizing their full humanity as well.

BEYOND PRO-LIFE VERSUS PRO-CHOICE

Many pro-life and pro-choice advocates have attempted to expand the definitions of "pro-life" and "pro-choice," respectively, but they are essentially trying to expand concepts that are inherently designed to exclude the experiences of most women, including poor women, women of color, Indigenous women, and women with disabilities. First, if we critically assess the assumptions behind both positions, it is clear that these camps are more similar than they are different. As I have argued, they both assume a criminal justice regime for adjudicating reproductive issues (although they may differ as to which women should be subjected to this regime). Neither position endows women with inherent rights to their bodies—the pro-life position pits the rights of unborn children against women's rights, whereas the pro-choice position argues

---

40. Camosy, *Beyond the Abortion Wars*, 17.

that women should have freedom to make choices rather than inherent rights to their body regardless of their class standing. They both support positions that reinforce racial and gender hierarchies that marginalize women of color and poor women. The pro-life position supports a criminalization approach that depends on a racist political system that will necessarily impact poor women and women of color who are less likely to have alternative strategies for addressing unwanted pregnancies.

Meanwhile, the pro-choice position often supports population-control policies and the development of dangerous contraceptives that are generally targeted in communities of color. Both positions do not question the larger systems of injustice that women face—they focus solely on whether a woman should have an abortion without addressing the economic, political, and social conditions that put women in this position in the first place. It is clear that a new approach is needed that does not focus on only one strategy for protecting the rights of women and their unborn children. Finding one requires us to rethink our relationship with the law and legal strategies for social change. In the next chapter I will suggest different possibilities grounded in the Bible for rethinking our relationship with the law.

CHAPTER 4

Rethinking the Law

AS DISCUSSED IN CHAPTER 2, the pro-life position equates promoting life with criminalization. This equation is based on the assumption that the best way to address a bad thing is to make it a crime. Essentially, we wish to make moral statements through the law, regardless of whether a particular law has the intended effect.

This chapter addresses an alternative approach. I suggest we should strategically engage the law rather than approaching it from a moral perspective. In fact, I would suggest that the Gospels actually present to us an alternative framework for engaging the law that can be particularly helpful in rethinking the criminalization of abortion. First, I will explore problematic assumptions made by evangelical scholars about what the Bible says about the criminalization of abortion. Then I explore alternative possibilities for understanding the biblical foundations for whether or not abortion should be criminalized. My goal is less to argue for a definitive interpretation and more to suggest that when we challenge our assumptions that respecting the lives of unborn children necessarily requires the criminalization of abortion, we may need to rethink what the Bible is actually calling us to do.

TRADITIONAL EVANGELICAL SCHOLARSHIP ON THE BIBLE AND ABORTION

Old Testament scholar James Hoffmeier notes in an important work he edited, *Abortion: A Christian Understanding and Response*, that the Old Testament does not actually say anything about abortion. Hoffmeier extrapolates that the Old Testament indirectly supports the criminalization of abortion because it supports the criminalization of child sacrifice. Of course, people who define themselves as "pro-choice" would also oppose child sacrifice. His argument is that while the Old Testament doesn't say anything about abortion, it does condemn sacrificing children. He contends that sacrificing children was the equivalent of abortion in Old Testament times because it was medically safer to sacrifice a child than to have an abortion. He also draws from Scriptures such as Jeremiah 1:5—"Before I formed you in the womb I knew you"—to argue that the Old Testament regarded the fetus as an unborn child and hence as a life.[1]

Victor Gordon notes that the New Testament makes no mention of abortion and is actually silent on whether or not the fetus is a life. He speculates that having a stance against abortion was so commonsensical that there was no reason to really speak on it. He also notes that many New Testament passages speak to the value of life. Again, however, we have no mandate on the criminalization of abortion, which is distinct from the value of life.[2]

Meanwhile, pro-choice advocates have argued that Exodus 21:22–25 suggests that the fetus is not a life, depending on how certain words are translated: "If people are fighting and hit a pregnant woman and she gives birth prematurely [or miscarries] but there is no serious injury, the offender must be fined whatever the woman's husband demands, and the court allows. But if there is serious injury, you are to take life for life, eye for eye, tooth for tooth, hand for hand, foot for foot, burn for burn, wound for wound, bruise for bruise." This suggests that miscarriage is not a serious

1. Hoffmeier, "Abortion."
2. Gordon, "Abortion."

injury. Pro-life scholars have argued that what is being described is not a miscarriage but a birth in which there is no injury. This could suggest that an actual miscarriage is considered a loss of life for which a life-for-a-life applies.

Michael Gorman helpfully goes through the biblical arguments both sides use to justify their positions. He notes that there is a tendency to prooftext—by presuming a certain position on abortion and then looking for passages that support that position, especially given that abortion is not directly addressed in the Bible. He argues for an approach that begins with the Bible, and that is open to exploring all the factors that might be related to abortion, including the status of women, what constitutes personhood, etc.[3]

Building on his argument, I note that most biblical arguments are based on the debate about when life begins. However, as I have argued previously, an answer to that question does not necessarily tell us whether or not we should support the criminalization of abortion as a strategy to promote life. Thus, in addition to looking to the Bible for guidance on when life begins, we might also want to look to the Bible for guidance on how we engage the law and strategies of criminalization. Here I suggest that the Gospels point to possible new directions for how we might engage the law.

THE CALL TO BE WISE AS SERPENTS

To orient ourselves with respect to the Bible and the law, it is important to remember that the Gospels were written by colonized people for colonized people under conditions of colonialism. This requires biblical writers to not only imagine the kingdom of God but to do so under conditions of coercion. Native studies scholar Scott Richard Lyons's work *X-Marks* points to a framework for how we can understand the Bible from the perspective of the colonized. He argues that treaty commissioners frequently had Native peoples sign treaties with an "x-mark." He describes the x-mark as "a sign of consent in a context of coercion" in which,

---

3. Gorman, "Use and Abuse."

despite the context of coercion, "there is always the prospect of slippage, indeterminacy, unforeseen consequences, or unintended results."[4] Essentially, the x-mark takes place within the context of colonialism, but it is a strategy and an attempt to survive the colonial context for a different kind of future.

Thus, could we possibly understand Mark 12:17 as an x-mark? "Give back to Caesar what is Caesar's and to God what is God's." This passage is often interpreted to mean that Jesus espoused political quietism and servitude. But what if we see this mandate as also an x-mark—written under conditions of colonialism that require strategic interventions to enable survival for a hope of a different kind of future? In fact, what if we read the Gospels in general as a survival text for living under conditions of colonialism? Doing so would suggest a different orientation to the law and political processes.

Drew Hart's *Who Will Be a Witness?* provides further guidance in this direction. In one chapter, he deeply reads Barabbas and argues that he has been misconstrued as an animalistic killer in many Christian traditions. Rather, he is more properly understood as a freedom fighter who was trying to liberate Israel from the Roman Empire and was willing to engage in violence to do so. Furthermore, Jesus's path, while distinct from Barabbas's, was not completely antagonistic to it either.[5] Through a nonviolent framework, Jesus seeks liberation for all in earthly and heavenly realms. Building on Hart's analysis, we could also understand Jesus as engaging in liberation strategically under conditions of colonialism. That is, a nonviolent approach could be supported not just on moral grounds but on strategic grounds if one is militarily completely outnumbered.

Indeed, Jesus explicitly advocates that his followers be strategic. As he states in Matthew 10:16, "Be ye therefore wise as serpents, and harmless as doves" (KJV). Similarly, Jesus prepares his followers for the fact that not all will listen to them. "If anyone will not welcome you or listen to your words, leave that home or town

4. Lyons, *X-Marks*, 3.
5. Hart, *Who Will Be*.

and shake the dust off your feet" (Matt 10:14). And elsewhere, Jesus notes that his followers may have to flee for their lives. "When you are persecuted in one place, flee to another" (Matt 10:23). Alexia Salvatierra and Peter Heltzel's *Faith-Rooted Organizing* discusses the importance of engaging in what they call dove and serpent power in advocating for social justice. As they state, organizing must be done in a manner that is cognizant of how systems of domination operate. "Jesus did not call us to be only innocent as doves, he also called us to be wise as serpents," they say, which requires us to not only act faithfully but to "act strategically."[6]

To be strategic does not mean forsaking principles altogether. As Jesus notes in Matthew 10, we can expect resistance, sometimes to the point of death, when we stand in the truth. Nonetheless, borrowing from Lyons's analysis, we are sharing the gospel in circumstances that are not of our choosing, and Jesus was most certainly sharing the gospel under conditions of oppression, colonialism, and violence. As a result, we must always think strategically about supporting biblical justice in a nonbiblical world, particularly when we come from communities with less access to social, economic, and political power.

ENGAGING THE LAW STRATEGICALLY

As I mentioned, we have a tendency to equate morality with the law. That is, we try to have the law make the moral statement we want to make. The problem is that sometimes, this can actually hinder the goals of that law. For instance, we criminalize abortion for the goal of promoting the life of unborn children. However, doing so can actually result in increased death for children and mothers.

But if we adopt the serpent power of Jesus with the understanding that we often work with legal systems that constrain what we can actualize, we might consider engaging the law strategically instead. In an unexpected place, antitrust law, we see a possible

---

6. Salvatierra and Heltzel, *Faith-Rooted Organizing*, 182.

direction that could inform how we engage the law strategically around abortion. In "Trust, Distrust, and Antitrust," Christopher Leslie proposes that antitrust law be reconceptualized for its strategic effects.[7] He notes that illegal cartels can have catastrophic impacts on economic markets and are difficult to combat. However, he notes that cartels are also unstable.[8] Because cartel members cannot develop formal relationships with each other, they must develop partnerships based on informal trust mechanisms to overcome the famous "prisoner's dilemma." As described by Leslie, this is a dilemma where two prisoners are arrested and questioned separately, with no opportunity for communication between them. There is enough evidence to convict both of minor crimes for a one-year sentence but not enough for a more substantive sentence. The police offer both prisoners the following deal: if you confess and implicate your partner, and your partner does not confess, you will be set free, and your partner will receive a ten-year sentence. If you confess, and he does as well, then you will both receive five-year sentences. In this scenario, it becomes the rational choice for both to confess because not confessing opens up the possibility of receiving a ten-year sentence if the other confesses. Ironically, however, while both will confess, both would be better off not confessing and receiving one-year sentences.

Similarly, Leslie argues, cartels face prisoner's dilemmas. If all cartel members agree to fix a price and abide by that price, then all will benefit. However, individual cartel members face the dilemma of whether to join the cartel and then cheat by lowering prices. They fear that someone else will drive them out of business if they do not cheat. At the same time, by cheating, they disrupt the cartel, which would have enabled all of them to profit with higher prices. In addition, they face a second dilemma when faced with antitrust legislation. Should they confess in exchange for immunity or take the chance that no one else will confess and implicate them?

---

7. Smith, "Moral Limits of the Law," for a more extended analysis of this approach.

8. Leslie, "Trust, Distrust, and Antitrust."

Unlike the classic prisoner's dilemma, however, cartel members have strategies to circumvent these pressures, including developing informal trust mechanisms. Such mechanisms include the development of personal relationships, frequent communication, goodwill gestures, etc. In the absence of trust, cartels may employ trust substitutes such as informal contracts, monitoring mechanisms, etc. When these trust and trust substitute mechanisms break down, the cartel members will start to cheat, thus causing the cartel to disintegrate.

Thus, Leslie proposes that antitrust legislation focuses on laws strategically disrupting these trust mechanisms. Unlike pro-life advocates who focus on making moral statements through the law, Leslie proposes using the law for strategic ends, even if the law makes a morally suspect statement. For instance, in his article "Antitrust Amnesty, Game Theory, and Cartel Stability," Leslie critiques the Department of Justice Antitrust Division's 1993 Corporate Leniency Program, which provided greater incentives for cartel partners to report on cartel activity. This policy provided "automatic" amnesty for the first cartel member to confess and decreased leniency for subsequent confessors in the order in which they confessed. This program led to an increase of amnesty applications.[9] However, Leslie notes that the ineligibility for amnesty of the cartel ringleader hindered the effectiveness of this reform. This policy seems morally sound. Why would we want the ringleader, the person who most profited from the cartel, to be eligible for amnesty? The problem with attempting to make a moral statement through the law is that it is counterproductive if the goal is to break up cartels. If the ringleader is never eligible for amnesty, the ring leader becomes inherently trustworthy within the cartel because he has no incentive to ever report on his partners. Through his inherent trustworthiness, the cartel can build its trust mechanisms. Thus, argues Leslie, the most effective way to destroy cartels is to render *all* members untrustworthy by granting all the possibility of immunity.

---

9. Leslie, "Antitrust Amnesty," 453–54.

What Leslie's analysis suggests is that an alternative framework for pursuing social change through the law is to employ it for its strategic effects rather than through the moral statements it purports to make. The pro-life movement has focused so singularly on reducing abortion by criminalizing it that they deem criminalization the correct moral strategy. When this strategy does not actually result in reducing abortions or causes negative unintended consequences, it becomes difficult to argue with it because it has been articulated as the moral choice. If, however, we were to focus on legal reforms chosen for their strategic effects, it would be easier to change the strategy if our calculus of its strategic effects were later proven incorrect. We would also be less complacent about the legal reforms we advocate, as has happened with most of the laws that have been passed on abortion. Pro-life advocates presume that because they helped pass a "moral" law, then their job is done. If, however, the criteria for legal reforms are their strategic effects, we would be continually monitoring the effects of these laws to see if they were having the desired effects.

For instance, as I previously mentioned, the anti-violence movement has been similar to the pro-life movement in that its primary strategy for ending domestic violence has been to focus on criminalization. Unfortunately, however, some of the laws passed by the anti-violence movement (such as mandatory arrest laws) have actually *increased* the death rate of domestic violence survivors. However because the anti-violence movement has focused on using the law to make a moral statement against domestic violence, it is now difficult to challenge these laws without sounding like a person who supports domestic violence.

But what if we focused on what will actually reduce domestic violence? For instance, since the primary reason domestic survivors do not leave battering relationships is that they do not have another home to go to, what if our legal strategies shifted from criminalizing domestic violence to advocating for affordable housing? Although the shift from criminalization may seem immoral, women are often removed from public housing under one-strike laws when a "crime" (including domestic violence) happens in their residence, whether or not they are the perpetrator. Thus, if our goal was actually to keep women safe, we might need to creatively rethink which legal reforms would actually increase safety.

Similarly, if we ask ourselves why women seek abortions, we might think strategically about which laws might address those underlying issues. For instance, if one reason why women seek abortions is that they cannot imagine raising a child with disabilities, then perhaps a legal reform that provides much greater support for families with disabled persons might decrease abortion rates. My point here is not to argue for a specific set of legislative changes but to suggest a different approach to the law. It is not enough to pass a law because it makes the moral statement we want. We must study the impact of the law to see what its effects are, and we must be willing to change our legal strategy if it has unanticipated negative impacts. In addition, focusing on making legal changes through strategic impacts can open more possibilities for engaging the law. We will be less likely to hold on to laws that hurt rather than help the causes they sought to promote.

THE LIMITS OF THE LAW

Ed Dobson and Cal Thomas's *Blinded by Might* provides a helpful framework for rethinking the proper relationship between Christians and the political process.[10] Dobson and Thomas, both former leaders of the Moral Majority, assert that the Religious Right fundamentally failed in its objectives because conservative Christians should not focus their energies upon the political process. Rather, their primary focus should be on religious conversion and cultural change. Legislative changes, they argue, accomplish little if the public at large does not support them.

Dobson and Thomas, of course, are not arguing that political and legal changes are irrelevant. However, they suggest that making far-ranging societal changes is difficult when we limit our strategies for social change to legal change. This is a reason why

---

10. Dobson and Thomas, *Blinded by Might*.

criminalizing abortion does not generally reduce abortion rates—because it does not attend to the reason why women feel pressured to have abortions in the first place. A multipronged approach is necessary to promote life for women and children.

Of course, the pro-life movement does not just engage in legal advocacy. It supports crisis pregnancy centers that attend to women's needs at best and attack women seeking abortions at worst. But generally, even these strategies are primarily focused on influencing a woman's decision after she has become unintentionally pregnant. In this respect, the pro-life movement is very similar to the pro-choice movement—both narrow their concern to influencing the decision whether or not to have an abortion. However, churches could do so much more by attending to the conditions that give rise to the difficult choices women have to make. In the next chapter, I will explore possibilities for a more holistic approach to abortion.

CONCLUSION

The pro-life movement has equated one particular legal strategy with a biblical and moral position on abortion. The result is that no space is created to work with others who may agree with the overall goal of preserving life but may disagree with that particular strategy. In addition, there is no opportunity to assess the effectiveness of that particular strategy to see if it actually protects the lives of unborn children without causing harm to women.

The Gospels indicate a different approach to legal reform that could be helpful for the pro-life movement. This approach does not imply a particular position for any legal issue. It suggests that if we look at the law not as the arbiter of morality but as one of many strategies, we can create the possibility for more open-ended and creative thinking that can further our vision.

In the Gospels, the extent to which Jesus actually runs afoul of the law is noteworthy. In Mark 2:3–28, the Pharisees constantly accuse Jesus of violating the law. But Jesus responds that their upholding the law contributes to negative results, such as people being ostracized from the kingdom of God or not receiving the healing they need. In fact, he was executed by the state with support from religious authorities. Does this mean Jesus thought the law was unimportant?

On the contrary, he suggested a different approach to the law. His critique of legal authorities was that they equated the law with justice and insisted on enforcing it even when it led to unjust results. Instead, the law is a tool or a strategy for justice. If a particular law does not lead to justice, it should be changed. In addition, the law is not the only way to bring about justice. Some principles that might emerge from assessing how Jesus engages the law include the following.

1. *Evaluate a law by its effects.* Jesus noted, "No good tree bears bad fruit, nor does a bad tree bear good fruit. Each tree is recognized by its own fruit. People do not pick figs from thornbushes, or grapes from briers" (Luke 6:43–44). Applied to the law, this means that a law that bears bad fruit is a bad law. Furthermore, Jesus suggests that we have a responsibility to look at the fruit of our actions. "Make a tree good and its fruit will be good, or make a tree bad and its fruit will be bad, for a tree is recognized by its fruit." Essentially, anyone can claim to be with God. But we know false prophets, false teachings, and false laws by their fruits.

Similarly, laws are passed in this country all the time that purport to make the world a better place. But that is not the end of our inquiry. We must always evaluate laws to see if they are, in fact, making the world a more just place.

2. *Focus on the spirit of the law.* In Mark 3:1–6, Jesus critiques a focus on legalism for its own sake.

> Another time, Jesus went into the synagogue, and a man with a shriveled hand was there. Some of them were looking for a reason to accuse Jesus, so they watched him closely to see if he would heal him on the Sabbath. Jesus said to the man with the shriveled hand, "Stand up in front of everyone."

> Then Jesus asked them, "Which is lawful on the Sabbath: to do good or to do evil, to save life or to kill?" But they remained silent.
> He looked around at them in anger and, deeply distressed at their stubborn hearts, said to the man, "Stretch out your hand." He stretched it out, and his hand was completely restored. Then the Pharisees went out and began to plot with the Herodians how they might kill Jesus.

We can see a corollary between the criminalization of abortion and Jesus's accusers' position on working on the Sabbath. The Pharisees, Jesus notes, are focused on the law rather than on the purpose of the law. Jesus states that the purpose of the Sabbath is to promote goodness and life. However, if an application of that law leads to death, then one must rethink that application. Similarly, the goal is not the criminalization of abortion per se but the promotion of justice and life. If criminalizing abortion does not actually further these goals, then we should at least be able to rethink that strategy.

I remember a similar phenomenon in my experience working in the anti-violence movement. I was at a conference on domestic violence where a facilitator asked us to imagine what we would like to see in twenty years. Everyone said things like more shelters, more anti-violence laws, etc. Not a single person said less domestic violence. It is very easy to become so committed to a particular strategy that we forget the larger vision that the strategy is supposed to further. People who may, in fact, agree with the vision but disagree with the strategy then become eternal enemies. We lose our ability to evaluate the strategy to see if it is actually working and to make strategic changes as necessary. In our commitment to a particular strategy, we can make bringing our vision to life more difficult.

Jesus, of course, does not say the law is not important or irrelevant. "Do not think that I have come to abolish the Law or the Prophets; I have not come to abolish them but to fulfill them" (Matt 5:17). He does not say, for instance, in Mark, to abolish the Sabbath. He calls not for the abolition of law but the fulfillment of it—to ensure that the application of law is actually achieving its purpose.

Similarly, if we approach legal reform from the perspective of strategy, we can constantly monitor our reforms to ensure that they are fulfilling their stated goals. The fact is that often, laws have negative, unintended consequences. But if we become less invested in legal strategies for their own sake and more invested in the world we want to bring into being through our legal strategies, then we will be more poised to correct mistakes and make changes in light of our vision. However, when we make a certain law, such as the criminalization of abortion, the goal in and of itself, then we can create collateral damage that is difficult to address and actually makes it difficult to adjust our course as needed because we have invested a particular legal strategy as *the* moral position.

Furthermore, when we singularly invest in legal strategies, we can close ourselves off to other strategies that might further our goal. By creating a broader-based strategy, we can engage people who may disagree on a particular strategy with other strategies that can further our goals. We may find that some strategies are more effective than legal strategies in changing the hearts and minds of the world. In the next chapter, I will explore other possibilities for protecting the lives of communities, women potentially seeking abortions, and their unborn children.

CHAPTER 5

Abortion Abolition

THE WORD "ABOLITION" HAS become a focal point in the controversial campaigns to defund the police. "Abolition" is often equated with scary radicals who want to burn everything down and is probably not a term the pro-life movement would willingly adopt. As I will explore later, there is much misunderstanding about the term's meaning. There are actually many insights from the defund-the-police movement that can assist those seeking a world without abortion, even if they do not agree with many of the movement's positions. At the same time, abolition has its own distinct history within evangelicalism that we might want to consider. By exploring the concept of abolition, I suggest that abortion abolition might be a more helpful framework than the current pro-life versus pro-choice paradigm. I will then explore some practical strategies for implementing abortion abolition.

ABOLITION AS THEOLOGY

> People are declaring that they are not content with living in a carceral state, and they are building a movement that has the potential to birth something novel, restorative, and transformative. We serve a God who desires liberation, reconciliation, and reintegration for those behind

bars. God invites the church to participate in setting the captives free.[1]

Penal abolition is not merely a decarceration programme, but also an approach, a perspective, a methodology, and most of all a way of seeing.[2]

Abolition is ultimately a theological project. By that, I mean it is not primarily about ending something; it is about replacing one system with a different system of relationality. It is thus a project of creating a different world that simultaneously transforms us into different persons who can live in this different world. I would define such a project as theological because it imagines a world beyond what is given or what can even be described—in short, the kingdom of God.

Pastor Jonathan Brooks of Canaan Community Church in Chicago uses architecture metaphorically to explain abolition theology. He notes that we tend to organize against things we oppose. However, the best approach is to view our situation as if we were architects. Architects start with the thing they want to build—the thing they want to bring into being in the world. Of course, to bring what they want into the world, things may have to be dismantled to clear the ground for the things they are building. But their actions are driven primarily by their positive vision rather than a negative vision.[3]

Brooks's analysis could be understood as an abolition theology. That is, abolition is primarily about creating the world we want to live in now. As we create this world, we may let things that are no longer needed pass away while making use of what we have, all the while focusing our energies on building systems that more closely image the kingdom of God.

Because abolition imagines worlds for which we have no words, as Vincenzo Ruggiero describes above, it is a methodology

---

1. Gilliard, *Rethinking Incarceration*, 199. Gilliard is director of racial righteousness and reconciliation for the Evangelical Covenant Church.

2. Ruggiero, "Abolitionist View," 100.

3. Brooks, "Race, Gender."

that is ever-evolving rather than one that offers a clear final destination—at least until Jesus returns, from an evangelical perspective. As the works of Angela Davis and Ruth Wilson Gilmore make clear in their focus on prison abolition, abolition cannot be reduced to a simple radical demand to end prisons (or end anything else, for that matter). Rather, it involves a political and organizing methodology for creating a world in which prisons would not be imaginable. In tracing the genealogy of the concept of "abolition," Davis contends that the abolition of slavery was limited by its lack of vision of what would replace a system of slavery. Building on the work of W. E. B. Du Bois, Davis notes that abolition required more than the negative project of ending formal slavery; it also required the positive project of creating democratic institutions that enabled the flourishing of Black life—hence abolition democracy.[4] Similarly, Davis argues that prison abolition must be a positive project: "Rather than try to imagine one single alternative to the existing system of incarceration, we might envision an array of alternatives that will require radical transformations of many aspects of our society."[5]

In practical terms, people often equate prison abolition with tearing all prison walls down tomorrow. But actually, it is more about creating new systems of care and safety that work more effectively than prisons or policing. Until we have those new systems, we must make the best of what we have. But abolition calls on us to go beyond reforming systems to imagining and creating new systems based on the principles of justice, fairness, and care. It asks us to go beyond being content with what we have to imagining what is truly just and transformative.

Furthermore, abolition requires not just the transformation of social relations and place but the transformation of ourselves. Abolition theology recognizes that we are all capable of both being harmed and harming others. It calls on us to create different systems of relationality that, in turn, transform us as people. Essentially, we must embark on a journey for which we have no

---

4. Davis, *Abolition Democracy*, 95.
5. Davis, *Are Prisons Obsolete?*, 108.

words that will result in the creation of new selves we would not now recognize.

While many might have major qualms about the prison abolition movement and its relationship to the defund-the-police movement, both movements offer many insights that we can utilize to develop an abortion abolition strategy. In addition, we can also be informed by how evangelicals have distinctly engaged abolition from a different trajectory. In the next section I explore how abolition has developed within evangelical thought and the connections between abolition within the defund movement and abolition within evangelical communities.

ABOLITION WITHIN EVANGELICALISM

The historical context for evangelical engagements with abolition begins with the racial reconciliation movement of the 1990s.[6] Evangelical complicity in slavery and racial segregation is well documented. Indeed, part of the genesis of the racial reconciliation movement entailed evangelicals coming to terms with the fact that, as former head of the Christian Coalition Ralph Reed admitted, the "white evangelical church carries a shameful legacy of racism."[7] Of course, Christian evangelicals also engaged in antislavery and racial justice struggles, but these numbers were fewer than those who used religion to defend racial hierarchies.

But in the 1990s, the Los Angeles riots, sparked by the acquittal of the police officers who assaulted Rodney King, spurred on white evangelicals to finally begin to address racism within evangelical churches. The evangelical men's movement the Promise Keepers made racial reconciliation part of its mission, and soon virtually every evangelical organization followed suit in what became known as the racial reconciliation movement. However, the movement addressed racism by promoting interracial relationships rather than by taking on institutionalized racism.

---

6. See Smith, *Unreconciled*, for an in-depth description of the movement; see Walker-Barnes, *Bring the Voices*, for a more insightful critique of the racial reconciliation movement.

7. Reed, *Active Faith*.

Nonetheless, even limited engagement with racism was significant, given the relative absence of antiracism work among white evangelicals previously.

At the same time, as mentioned previously, evangelicals became increasingly involved in prison reform through the work of Charles Colson and Prison Fellowship. Prison and Justice Fellowship and other evangelical prison advocates supported, implicitly or explicitly, decarceration for drug offenders;[8] minimum wage compensation for prison labor; decarceration of all nonviolent offenders ("The first thing we have to do with prisons today is to get the non-violent people out");[9] prison construction moratoriums;[10] eradication of "zero tolerance" policies in public schools;[11] eradication of mandatory-minimum sentencing and three-strikes legislation; decarceration of the mentally ill;[12] suffrage for convicted felons;[13] expansion of community-sentencing programs;[14] and even prison abolition to a very limited degree.[15]

Despite the work of Prison Fellowship and other evangelical prison-organizing movements, as well as work done under the auspices of racial reconciliation, the word "abolition" became associated, not with prison abolition, as it has in more secular social justice circles, but with anti-trafficking organizing within evangelical circles.

An exhibit proclaiming, "I am an Abolitionist. Are you?" from InterVarsity Press, an evangelical publisher, at the 2013 Justice Conference (an annual conference held for evangelicals mobilizing for social justice), called on conference participants not to

---

8. Colson, "Prison Reform," 52; Bruce, "More than Jailhouse Religion"; Colson, "Who Will Help," 17.

9. Forbes, "What Hope," 33; Smarto, *Setting the Captives Free*, 46.

10. Colson, "God behind Bars," 29; Mill, "No Prisons in Heaven"; Justice Fellowship, *Jubilee Extra*, 1–3; Van Ness, "Crisis."

11. Nolan, "Justice e-Report."

12. Nolan, "Two New Laws."

13. Colson, "God behind Bars," 34.

14. Colson, "God behind Bars," 29; Pulliam, "Better Idea than Prison."; Van Ness, "Crisis."

15. Griffith, *Fall of the Prison*.

become involved in prison reform but to join the anti-trafficking movement. InterVarsity holds a weeklong program called the Abolitionist Plunge, with the goal to immerse students "in every aspect of the fight against human trafficking, or modern-day slavery. During the course of the week, students hear from trafficking survivors, volunteer with local organizations that are fighting against human trafficking, and learn about a God who wants to set all His children free."[16] The program's slogan is "Become a Modern Day Abolitionist."[17]

Thus, while the prison abolition movement has generally tried to connect legacies of anti-Black racism from slavery through incarceration, in the evangelical abolition movement, trafficking supplants the legacy of chattel slavery, as in the assertion that "during the last two decades worldwide human trafficking totals surpass that of 400 years of colonial slavery by a million."[18] In fact, trafficking is often described in a manner that erases the importance of chattel slavery. "Today 27 million people live on in captivity, their lives worth far less than any colonial era slave."[19] Anti-trafficking is described as the "new abolition movement."[20] In fact, *Relevant* magazine published an article entitled "U.S. Slave Traffic" that does not address slavery's connection to anti-blackness at all.[21] This rhetorical strategy follows from the fact that those guilty of the "new slavery" are generally people of color, and the rescuers of enslaved women are usually white, thus erasing historical connections between racism and slavery.[22] Or, as Lyndsey P. Beutin notes,

---

16. Anderson, "Fighting," para. 2.

17. Anderson, "Fighting."

18. Powell, "America's Ugliest Crime," 40. See also Olasky, "Life of a Slave"; Justice, "Setting the Sex-Trafficked Captives."

19. Abraham, "Let My People Go!" para. 1.

20. Alford, "Free at Last." See also Blunt, "Devil's Yoke."; Beaty, "Portland's Quiet Abolitionist."

21. "Tracking the Rise."

22. Powell, "America's Ugliest Crime"; Scimone, "Stop Child Slavery Now"; Jewell, "Red Light Rescue"; Abraham, "Abolitionist"; Price, "Day Slavery Ended."

the anti-trafficking movement reduces slavery of Black people to a "usable past."[23]

SHIFTS IN EVANGELICAL ABOLITION

Evangelical scholar Soong-Chan Rah penned a "cry to not derail the prophetic call of #blacklivesmatter with all lives matter":

> It was not ALL lives that were ripped from their homes in Africa....
> It was not ALL lives that were bought and sold by God-fearing white American Christians.
> It was not ALL lives that were whipped and beaten on the plantations....
> It was not ALL lives that were told "separate but equal" with equal never being equal....
> It was not ALL lives that have been victims of police violence, but it was the black life of Oscar Grant.
> It was not ALL lives, it was the black life of Trayvon Martin.
> It was not ALL lives, it was the black life of Michael Brown.
> It was not ALL lives, it was the black life of John Crawford, Eric Garner, Tamir Rice, Freddie Gray, Sandra Bland....
> It is not ALL lives that the prison industrial complex exploits.
> These historical events did not involve the destruction and death of ALL lives, they were black lives that have been systematically targeted and abused by American society.
> So next time, white evangelical leaders, you feel the urge to mouth off that "ALL Lives Matter"—CLOSE your mouth and OPEN your eyes, ears, and minds to get yourself some knowledge.[24]

---

23. Beutin, "Black Suffering."
24. Rah, "Soong-Chan Rah Says."

People of color involved in the evangelical racial reconciliation movement started calling for a shift from racial reconciliation to racial justice in the wake of (1) the rise of the Black Lives Matter movement and (2) the election of Donald Trump.

As Soong-Chan Rah's quote exemplifies, many evangelicals of color began to intensify their efforts against police violence and mass incarceration in reaction to the Black Lives Matter movement. Building on the prior work of organizations like Prison Fellowship, this work more explicitly centered on the analysis of anti-Black racism and focused on problems with the system. And Prison Fellowship itself has focused more on racism in the legal system. Many evangelicals were involved in the organizing in Ferguson, Missouri, which in turn increased their interest in criminal justice reform.

Dominique Gilliard's *Rethinking Incarceration* reflects this shift in evangelical organizing against policing and prisons. Gilliard does not explicitly espouse an abolitionist position in this book. But his interlocutors are abolitionists, and he works with the Christian Community Development Association's Mass Incarceration Task Force, which does explicitly engage abolition. His critiques of incarceration go far beyond those of previous evangelical engagements with prison reform by arguing that incarceration itself is based on "dehumanization, exploitation and profiteering."[25] Further, rather than position evangelical theology as the antidote to the problems of incarceration, Gilliard calls on evangelicals to decarcerate their theology. Incarceration "is a byproduct of the church's failure to sustain a witness that subverts the power of empire. . . . It is evidence of what transpires when the church forgets its mission, ceases its prophetic witness, and cowers before imperial power."[26]

As Gilliard's work suggests, abolition as a methodology informs not only the increasing insistence by evangelicals of color of the need to focus on policing and prisons but also their insistence on questioning the frameworks of white evangelicalism itself. With

25. Gilliard, *Rethinking Incarceration*, 191.
26. Gilliard, *Rethinking Incarceration*, 189.

the majority of white evangelicals voting for President Trump, who seemed to personify none of the values white evangelicals previously claimed to prioritize, many evangelicals of color began to conclude that white evangelicals value their whiteness more than Jesus. Consequently, increasingly more evangelicals of color are asking the question, is evangelicalism itself an inherently colonial and racial project? An example can be found in the conference statement for the Liberating Evangelicalism: Decentering Whiteness Conference that took place in Chicago in September 2019:

> Christian evangelicalism, particularly of late, has often been equated with partisan politics and the faulty assumption that all evangelicals are white. Liberating Evangelicalism seeks to challenge this assumption by creating a space for a biblically-based, people of color centered movement that is open to all who seek to build a Jesus-centered vision for social justice. We imagine a space where people of color are at the center rather than the margins of the conversation, a place to build visions of liberation and inclusion, and a place for belonging and community-building with peoples across diverse political and theological perspectives.
>
> By "liberating evangelicalism," however, this conference does not presume a particular attachment to Christian evangelicalism. Some may seek to reclaim the term "evangelical" while others, suspicious of its history and contemporary expression, intend to jettison it from their faith identity altogether. We seek to create a space that allows for diverse engagements with biblically-rooted faith traditions. In building this space, this gathering also does not presume any particular theological or political perspectives.[27]

This organizing is in many ways distinct from the histories of more white-dominated progressive evangelical organizing in that it does not claim to replace a "bad" conservative evangelicalism with a "good" progressive evangelicalism but instead calls for a theological and political enterprise based on uncertainty. In

---

27. See the conference website at www.liberatingevangelicalism.org.

fact, several speakers at the conference, such as AnaYelsi Sanchez-Velasco and Ken Fong, argued that evangelicalism could not be liberated, and Michal Mata argued that he was now an "evangelical atheist" because he could no longer support that which had been packaged as evangelicalism. Others, such as Soong-Chan Rah, argued that white evangelicalism was more invested in whiteness than in Jesus and hence was not actually evangelical at all. And Michelle Higgins explicitly articulated an abolitionist policy that made the connections between evangelical and prison abolition. She argued that evangelical theology fundamentally challenges white supremacist notions of "innocence." That is, evangelicalism recognizes that no one is more pure than anyone else. All are in need of grace and redemption. Or, as evangelical activist Shane Claiborne articulated at the 2019 Christian Community Development Association conference, "No one is beyond reproach or redemption." Consequently, one must reject incarceration because it is a punishment strategy that presumes that some are less "innocent" than others and, hence, are disposable.

Another example can be found in an essay by Erna Kim Hackett: "Why I Stopped Talking about Racial Reconciliation and Started Talking about White Supremacy." She, as well as many other evangelicals of color, makes the critique that white evangelicals reduce the analysis of race to interpersonal relationships rather than address institutionalized forms of racism. But she further gestures to the problem with evangelical theology itself.

> Secondly, white Christianity suffers from a bad case of Disney Princess Theology. As each individual reads Scripture, they see themselves as the princess in every story. They are Esther, never Xerxes or Haman. They are Peter, but never Judas. They are the woman anointing Jesus, never the Pharisees. They are the Jews escaping slavery, never Egypt. For the citizens of the most powerful country in the world, who enslaved both Native and Black people, to see itself as Israel and not Egypt when it is studying Scripture, is a perfect example of Disney Princess Theology. It also means that as people in power, they have no lens for locating themselves rightly in Scripture

or society—and it has made them blind and utterly ill-equipped to engage issues of power and injustice.[28]

Her work indicates this larger impulse to critically deconstruct the terms of white evangelicalism. It suggests that the process of decentering whiteness within evangelicalism may result in surprising outcomes. It coalesces around a commitment toward an open-ended theological praxis and process rather than a commitment to a bounded set of theological and political principles. Or, to quote Daniel J. Camacho, it resists the politics of theological stop-and-frisk. Does that mean evangelicalism has no boundaries at all? No, but it suggests another approach to boundaries. Evangelical theologian Paul Metzger borrows from missiologist Paul Hiebert's work to differentiate between bounded and centered sets as models for defining evangelicalism. A bounded set focuses on static boundaries to define who is in and who is out. A centered set focuses on core evangelical beliefs but is less concerned with excluding those who fall outside a certain boundary.[29] By remaining in conversation with people with whom we disagree, we are in a greater position to make changes we need to make as God's word to us becomes apparent.

The far-reaching impact of this evangelical abolitionist stream was evident in the Ethics and Religious Liberty Commission (ERLC) of the Southern Baptist Convention (SBC) conference, Caring Well, held in Dallas in October 2019. This conference was organized to address the abuse crisis in Southern Baptist churches that was publicly exposed by the *Houston Chronicle*.[30] A series of articles chronicled the countless number of survivors of abuse in SBC churches and institutions, which has gone unaddressed for decades. This conference was noteworthy in the far-reaching critique of the SBC made by speakers, including those in leadership, given that the SBC is not known for radical politics. Russell Moore, the head of the ERLC, argued that abuse proliferates when churches

---

28. Hackett, "Why I Stopped Talking," para. 11.
29. Metzger, *Connecting Christ*.
30. See Downen et al., "Abuse of Faith."

think abuse always happens in churches that have the "wrong" theology. Abusers are often the most theologically correct, contended Moore. Diana Langberg, a psychologist, argued that the abuse crisis in the SBC can be connected to the fact that the denomination was created in defense of slavery and hence was "rotten to the core." Phillip Bethancourt, vice president of the ERLC, claimed that the question on the table was not how the SBC should address the crisis but whether the SBC continues to exist at all. And Boz Tchvidijian (founder of GRACE, which organizes around abuse in churches) stated that the SBC "system is broken." He stated that if kids were being murdered inside SBC churches and a newspaper wrote an exposé about it, "either the entire denomination would implode or the entire system would have to be dismantled."[31] He likened sexual abuse to the murder of children. He also specifically called on the SBC to renounce its male-dominated structures. Beth Moore similarly called on the SBC to renounce its complicity in "misogyny." Chris Moles argued that the SBC needed to fundamentally question its power structures, in which pastors have unquestioned authority. As Beth Moore similarly stated, "Those who cannot be questioned cannot be trusted."[32]

And it should be noted that the SBC and the Gospel Coalition organized an entire conference on racism at the 2015 ERLC Leadership Summit that addressed institutionalized racism as well as police violence against people of color very pointedly.[33] Russell Moore began the conference by arguing "why racial reconciliation is a gospel issue."[34] He stated that while we know the faces and names of the men who started the SBC, "no one knows the names of the enslaved men and women who were kidnapped to work the fields of some of those men. . . . No one memorializes the names of the women who were raped and the families who were split apart often by people who knew how to preach on family values."[35] And

---

31. Briggs, "Boz Tchividjian to SBC," para. 3.
32. Jenkins, "In Dallas," para. 12.
33. Graham, "Southern Baptists."
34. Lee, "Life after Prison," 46.
35. Smith, *Unreconciled*.

a year later, the ERLC included criminal justice reform on its 2016 legislative agenda for the first time. The ability of the prophetic voices within the SBC can be a model for courageously engaging in self-critique as we aim to be closer to God's vision for the world.

ABOLITION AS METHODOLOGY

Abolition theology requires rethinking the division between "sinners and saints." In stating that he "came for sinners, not for saints," Jesus articulated that the church is not a space to affirm us as we are but a place to enable us to become something different from what we are. Thus, Jesus's command to have a church for sinners is actually also a critique of liberation movements. That is, liberation theologies have often positioned God as really being on the side of the "oppressed" rather than the "oppressor." But the concept of a church of sinners indicates that God stands against oppression, no matter who commits it. There is no pure community before God—we are churches of sinners, and hence, we need to develop church communities that engage in continual and humble self-critique and interrogation to ascertain when, even with good intentions, we may be hurting others. To quote Eugene Cho: "We ask God to move mountains without considering we may need to be the mountain that needs to be moved."[36]

But it is not only evangelicals who could benefit from abolition methodologies. In more secular social justice circles, there is often a divide between those deemed to have sufficiently progressive politics, and those thought lacking such views. But abolition methodology recognizes that no one emerges unscathed from the human race, having lived thousands of years in understructures of racial, economic, and political injustice. Russell Moore stated at the 2016 ERLC conference in his critique of white nostalgia that was part of the Trump "Make America Great Again" campaign, "When we say we need to go back to before everything fell apart,

---

36. Cho, plenary speech, Justice Conference.

that would mean going back to Genesis 3."[37] Our visions of the world are so fundamentally structured through living under normalized conditions of injustice that even if we feel we have better politics than another person, we still have terrible politics that we have not yet realized.

I was once teaching a class in which we discussed Trump's advocacy of a wall at the United States/Mexico border. All the students in my class were critical of this policy and argued that it was an example of racism. I asked my students what they would say to someone who voted for Trump *because of* his policy on the border wall. They all said they wouldn't even try to talk to that person because all Trump supporters are hopeless. I then asked them if they had always had the political positions they currently have and, if not, what had changed their mind. As it turns out, about half of the students had been Trump supporters the year before. But now they had trouble even talking to their former selves. But if we are actually following Jesus, we should expect to change our views constantly and realize everyone around us is also a work in progress.

Abolition as a methodology is something that is essential for all social justice movements. Abolition is not primarily about the end of a bad thing (be it prisons, abortion, trafficking, etc.); it is an end to the world as we know it and an end to ourselves as we know them so that we become new creatures in Christ capable of living in God's kingdom. Such a journey requires more than having the correct political or theological positions; it requires courage and commitment to embark on a collective journey into uncertainty.

Churches should be an ideal place to do this work. That is social justice work, particularly the work of racial reconciliation, is often framed as a relatively simple task within evangelical circles. Conservatives tend to focus on racism as an interpersonal issue and strive to develop cross-cultural friendships. Liberals tend to focus on racism as a structural issue and strive to develop policies or laws to correct racial injustice. However, as Frederick Moten has stated, "White supremacy is not simply about the belief in white

---

37. Smith, *Unreconciled*.

superiority, white supremacy structures belief itself."[38] That is, racism also operates on the ontological level. Racism and other forms of social injustice fundamentally structure who we are (compliments of original sin), what we can ever perceive, and what we can imagine as being possible. But of course, God is God "of the impossible" rather than "of the possible," and his kingdom is far beyond our imagination. Thus, God's vision for justice is a scary and difficult enterprise because it requires us to go from a place of certainty to a place of perpetual uncertainty. We must have faith in the "substance of things hoped for," a world for which we have no words and for the new selves that will emerge, which we would not recognize today. Many liberals castigate Trump supporters for their views on race and deem them uneducated on a variety of issues. This tends to assume that all people voted for Trump for the same reason. In addition, the presumption is that the fundamental issue is that Trump supporters lack education, and hence, the antidote is more education. However, the negative reaction against much social justice work is often based on ontology rather than lack of information. That is, many people correctly perceive that social justice work fundamentally changes the world as we know it and ourselves as we know it. It is to embark on a journey of uncertainty and instability. And often, the bad that is known is better than the good that is not known. Thus, as Daniel Hill notes, this work is ultimately pastoral rather than educational. How do we create faith communities of care that enable us to collectively go through this journey together; where we don't just receive information from a two-hour antiracism seminar but actually create collective spaces to work through our challenges, fears, and anxieties while co-creating God's kingdom together?

TOWARD ABORTION ABOLITION

Now, what does abolition have to do with abortion? The philosophies undergirding abolition, including prison abolition, can

---

38. Frederick Moten, Class Lecture, UC Riverside, April 2, 2014. Originally cited in Smith, "Evangelicals," 1.

inform our approach to abortion in some ways. First, as I have discussed previously, an abolition approach would cause us to question whether criminalization is the best way to end abortion. Second, it would inspire us to focus less on the negative aspect of simply ending abortion and more on what systems would need to be in place so abortion was not something people even thought about. Like prison abolition, abortion abolition would be a positive project in which we could create new social systems and systems of care in which no one was disposable. Churches could ideally be centers to create these new systems, which could be models for the world to follow. In addition, an abolition approach could provide more opportunities for people to work together across the pro-life versus pro-choice divide because we would be less focused on battling over a particular strategy and more concerned with cooperatively imagining the world that would ensure the care of all people.

PUTTING ABORTION ABOLITION INTO PRACTICE

How can we put abortion abolition into practice? Abortion abolition is a creative and imaginative process. It begins by (1) considering what conditions give rise to women being in the position of considering an abortion, and (2) imagining what the world would have to be like for women not to end up in this position. In addition, it engages in a harm-reduction strategy. That is, until we have the world we would like, how can we reduce the harm in the meantime? Consequently, there is not a clear prescription of what approaches to take. We must experiment and try different approaches as we learn from our mistakes and the mistakes of others.

I have taught many abortion workshops and classes with people from pro-life and pro-choice perspectives. As a thought exercise, I ask people to suspend their political positions on whether or not they think abortion should be criminalized. I then ask, what else can be done to both reduce abortion and promote the lives of women who might be seeking abortions? I have generally found that once the criminalization debate is suspended, people have no trouble thinking of strategies they can agree on. This process then enables people to stop seeing each other as an "enemy" and to start seeing others as people they can work with on at least some strategies. So, one possibility for groups working across the pro-life/pro-choice divide is to see what people can agree on.

Below are some suggestions that people across the divide have considered as ways to address this issue. I offer them less as a prescription and more as a stimulus to spark our collective imagination of what else might be possible. Some strategies you may fervently agree with. There may be other amazing strategies not on this list. Some strategies might work in one context but not in another. Some strategies might have to be modified and adapted. But the point is to go beyond the one narrow strategy of criminalization/legalization to focus on all the things that might enable a better world for women, their unborn children, and their communities.

One way to think about how to get to the conditions that give rise to abortion is to ask ourselves why a woman, even one who might consider herself pro-life, would seek one. And then, given these reasons, what else can be done?

DEVELOPING A HARM-REDUCTION APPROACH TO NONMARITAL SEX

Churches often shame women who become pregnant while unmarried. Thus, to avoid this shaming, they will seek an abortion. Thus, it might be necessary to create structures and processes that send the message that single women who become pregnant will be welcomed and embraced. This is counter to what we see in churches, however, because such an approach would be seen as condoning nonmarital sex. In the next section, I will argue for an alternative way of imagining the church as a church of sinners; this might enable churches to more effectively address internal issues while retaining their principles.

Part of this entails integrating families with single parents more fully into the church so that single women who are pregnant can imagine life after the birth of their child within the church rather than having to leave the church or seek an abortion.

In addition, a harm-reduction approach might provide more access to contraceptive counseling to prevent unwanted pregnancies, especially for teenagers. Of course, such a strategy contradicts what many churches teach regarding abstinence. However, here, churches could be informed by harm-reduction practices around drug addiction. Harm reduction recognizes that while drug addiction is not a good thing, it also exists. By engaging in harm reduction, it is possible to increase the likelihood that those with addictions will not die before they have the opportunity to overcome their addictions.

Similarly, as discussed previously, despite church teachings to the contrary, evangelical teens are having premarital sex at the same rate as other teens. Providing contraceptive information might stop a teen from feeling she needs to have an abortion in order to save face in the church. Providing this information can coexist with teachings on abstinence without sanctioning premarital sex itself.

Part of a harm-reduction approach involves nondirective counseling. Many women who become pregnant seek counseling from a pro-life counseling center. However, because the counseling is so directed and does not really allow women to fully explore all their options, they often have no choice but to go to a pro-choice center to do so. But those centers are geared toward directing women toward an abortion. Ironically, then, the directed counseling within crisis pregnancy centers can set women up to get abortions because they end up going from one directed-counseling venue to another. In addition, because a great number of abortions are repeat abortions, such women lose their connections to alternative possibilities for unwanted pregnancies. This might be why evangelicals are more likely than other people to have repeat abortions.[39]

Care Net found that women seeking abortions rarely go to their church for advice. One reason is that they expect to receive

---

39. Care Net, *Study of Women*.

condemnation rather than support, and in fact, do receive condemnation rather than support.[40] Thus, having a very directed approach toward abortion actually makes it more likely women will exclude themselves from the church altogether and hence receive less church guidance on their decision.

Instead, some evangelicals have advocated establishing counselors within the church who appear more neutral in their faith communities to allow women to fully wrestle with all the issues they need to address. In this way, women may be able to come up with a life plan that meets their needs. In addition, they have argued that it is important for such counselors to affirm the decision a woman makes, even if it is for abortion. That way, if the relationship is maintained, a woman is more likely to come back if a future unwanted pregnancy happens, and thus, it is more likely she will make a different decision next time.

PROVIDING HOLISTIC SUPPORT FOR WOMEN WHO HAVE UNWANTED PREGNANCIES THROUGH THE CHILD'S LIFE SPAN

Many women have complained to me that when they went to a crisis pregnancy center, they felt that they were shamed into keeping their pregnancy but were given no support for the care of their child. If they were given support, it was usually limited to getting diapers or baby clothes.

As mentioned previously, a wealth of ministries do provide material support for women facing unwanted pregnancies. However, a woman facing an unwanted pregnancy is not just thinking about how she will get through the pregnancy or the first year of the baby's born life; she is wondering how she can get through the next eighteen years of that life. She asks herself whether the baby will prevent her from securing the job or education she needs to sustain herself and any future children. Thus, if churches could

---

40. Care Net, *Study of Women*.

demonstrate ongoing support for women, having a child, which might have seemed unimaginable at first, might now seem possible.

DEVELOPING CHURCH MINISTRIES THAT FULLY SUPPORT AND INTEGRATE PEOPLE WITH DISABILITIES

One reason people seek abortions is that they find that their child is going to have a disability. Because we have an ableist society, it is often perceived that it is better to be dead than disabled. Furthermore, there is a lack of resources for families to care for children with disabilities. As a result, even if parents value a child with a disability, they might wonder if they will have the resources to support that child.

Churches do not often focus on people with disabilities. First, many churches are not very accessible on multiple levels. They may not have wheelchair access; their programs may not be tailored for the visually impaired; there may be no ASL (American Sign Language) interpretation; etc. One man who was often hired as a church musician told me that he was gay. But he was also in a wheelchair. He said he had been hired in many conservative congregations, but he received more hostility for being in a wheelchair than he did for being gay because the churches did not want to accommodate his disability or they feared his wheelchair would mess up their floors.

To the extent that a disability is considered in church settings, it is usually seen as a "ministry" to help poor, disabled people. People with disabilities are not often imagined as having something to contribute to the church or being qualified to serve in church leadership; rather, they are seen as objects of pity.

If people with disabilities were more fully centered in the life of the church in all areas and if families with disabilities were provided the full support they need, it would no longer seem like a daunting endeavor to give birth to a child with a disability. As Amos Yong argues, if we read the Gospels through a non-ableist lens, we can see that people with disabilities are central to the

Gospels and Jesus's ministry. "The goal cannot be just to minister to [people with disabilities] as objects of care, concern, or charity . . . the goal must be the full inclusion of all and the reception of each contribution, resulting in the enrichment and edification of others."[41] When we create such a community, giving birth to children with disabilities will no longer be feared.

ENDING SEXUAL AND DOMESTIC VIOLENCE

Many unwanted pregnancies come from a condition of coercion. A woman struggling with an unwanted pregnancy may be concurrently struggling under conditions of violence, thus increasing the likelihood that abortion may feel necessary as a matter of survival. Girls who are sexually abused are more likely to become pregnant as teenagers.[42] Intimate-partner violence during pregnancy increases the likelihood a woman will seek an abortion. Sexual assault is also a part of domestic violence that can increase unwanted pregnancy. Sexual assault, in general, can always result in pregnancy. It thus makes sense to end sexual and domestic violence to reduce the abortion rate.

Unfortunately, as the recent scandals in the Southern Baptist Convention and other church denominations indicate, churches have not been healing places for addressing sexual or domestic violence and have often created conditions that proliferate abuse. The focus on male headship in marriage can promote the idea that women lack autonomy over their own bodies. As Camden Morgante notes, the impact of purity culture can also have the unintended consequence of making it difficult to talk about not only nonmarital sex but also sexual abuse.[43] In fact, some studies have indicated that the presence of religious fundamentalism

---

41. Yong, *Bible, Disability*, 79.
42. Stock et al., "Adolescent Pregnancy."
43. Morgante, "5 Purity Culture Myths."

is the second-best predictor of sexual abuse in the home (next to alcoholism).[44]

The first step in addressing sexual and domestic violence in the church is to acknowledge that it exists. To give one example, when I was working as a crisis counselor, I was in a group that was organizing around domestic violence in churches. One pastor said that domestic violence was not an issue in his church. So, he was challenged to just briefly mention the issue in a sermon. At the next meeting, he reported that he mentioned domestic violence in his sermon, and afterward, over fifty women in his congregation sought his counsel because they were in a domestic violence situation.

Thankfully, more and more people are speaking out about sexual violence in the church through the increased visibility of #ChurchToo and #MeToo. Strategies for addressing these issues could fill another book. But I will briefly state that the first thing to addressing sexual violence in the church is to assume that it is prevalent rather than an aberration. If we assume it is prevalent, then we must address the structural issues in the church that allow it to occur by asking the following questions:

1. Is there a culture of unquestioned authority in the church?
2. Are there insufficient accountability mechanisms in the church should a leader engage in abuse?
3. Is there a culture of silence around these issues?
4. Are abuse allegations swept under the rug, or are those who are abused encouraged to forgive and forget without attention to their safety?
5. Does the church not center the safety of survivors?
6. Does church functioning depend on the goodness of its leaders rather than on the soundness of its processes?

I will address question 6 in more detail in the next section. But overall, there is a tendency to presume that when abuse is

---

44. Heggen, *Sexual Abuse*.

revealed, it's just one bad person that we need to expel. But the reality is that churches are hotbeds of abuse because the structures enable it. We tend to want to build the church around the "right people" rather than the "right processes." The result is that when that "right" person causes harm, no processes are available to catch the behavior or course-correct. And when people are given too much power, it is likely they will abuse that power. In Matthew 23:8–12, Jesus says: "But you are not to be called 'Rabbi,' for you have one Teacher, and you are all brothers. And do not call anyone on earth 'father,' for you have one Father, who is in heaven. Nor are you to be called instructors, for you have one Instructor, the Messiah. The greatest among you will be your servant. For, those who exalt themselves will be humbled, and those who humble themselves will be exalted." Essentially, Jesus is calling for a different model of leadership that is less hierarchical and, hence, less vulnerable to abuse. Churches can be places where we not only appropriately respond to harm but also create new processes and structures that stop harm from happening in the first place.

DEVELOPING A CHURCH FOR SINNERS

A harm-reduction approach often seems counter to Christian principles because the presumption is that Christians need to model exemplary behavior. Pregnancy as a result of premarital sex is, according to John Piper, an indication of sin (even if the pregnancy itself is not sin).[45] Because women do not want to feel they are walking signs of sin, many Christian women will have abortions to avoid public shaming.

However, if we look at the model of Jesus's ministry, we see that he did not actually hang around exemplary people. He associated with tax collectors, sinners, etc., and was constantly questioned for his associations. He was not afraid to look bad. His response: "It is not the healthy who need a doctor, but the sick.

---

45. Piper, "Is It Sinful."

I have not come to call the righteous, but sinners to repentance" (Luke 5:31–32).

We have seen the problems time and time again where Christian leaders have a morally exemplary public face while engaging in abusive or immoral behavior privately. However, the tendency is to individualize this phenomenon. That church "just" had the misfortune of having a "bad" pastor or spiritual leader. But when there is this much abuse in the church and this much inconsistency between private and public behavior, we have to ask ourselves the question, is there something in the way our faith communities are structured that is giving rise to this problem?

Jesus's model of ministry points to what may be an issue. The fact is that we are all highly flawed human beings because we have grown up with structures of sin, injustice, and violence. Making a decision for Christ does not eliminate all our flaws because we have been so structured by the logic of sin and injustice. To be a Christian is to become a fundamentally different person in Christ—it is not just having the correct theological beliefs. And becoming a fundamentally different person is actually not that easy. "Therefore, if anyone is in Christ, he is a new creation. The old has passed away; behold, the new has come" (2 Cor 5:17 ESV). It requires building community practices around the people we actually are rather than idealized versions of ourselves.

This is what Jesus did. He built a community around people as they were, a community where people did not have to hide their problems and flaws, but he built practices that enabled them to change over time. Similarly, we could rethink churches as places for sinners who are welcomed as they are but who get support to transform themselves over time.

Currently, when a person is struggling with an issue that the church does not support, such as premarital sex, that person has no other option than to hide the struggle to remain in the church. Because that issue remains hidden, the person gets no support, thus ensuring that the issue will only grow. But if there was space to be honest about our issues, where we knew we would still be welcomed and supported, warts and all, then we could be honest about our struggles. This would enable churches to develop practices that allow us to work through our struggles.

Now, the question arises: would such an approach enable abuse or immoral behavior? It certainly could. The recent media coverage of the rampant sexual abuse committed in Southern Baptist churches illustrates what happens when churches do not seriously address abuse. In these cases, however, one of the reasons the abuse proliferated was that allegations of abuse were silenced and not made public. As a result, no practices were put in place to ensure the safety of survivors or create anything that would enable people to change. In addition, being a church of sinners does not eliminate restrictions on a particular role a person might play in that community. For instance, if a person has a history of financial mismanagement, the church may not allow that person anywhere near a bank account. But that does not mean the person cannot be anywhere at all. In a serious case of abuse, the safety of church members might mean an abuser is banned from attending church services. But that does not mean the abuser could not be anywhere at all. The abuser might be in a separate, connected community for people who struggle with abuse.

A great number of abortions would not happen in evangelical churches if evangelical women who faced an unwanted pregnancy knew they would still be loved, accepted, and supported if their pregnancy and the circumstances behind it were made public. To be loved, accepted, and supported does not necessarily mean accepting behaviors, but it means truly embracing the person while supporting her along the process of choosing new behaviors in the future.

LISTENING

Some of the suggestions I have offered come from listening sessions I have participated in. However, as a methodology, a church could form its own listening sessions. It might do anonymous surveys to sound out people who might otherwise be afraid to speak publicly about their feelings. It could do focus groups or many other strategies, where the goal is just to listen without judgment. After truly listening, churches may find it easier to develop innovative strategies to address their needs. Such processes would enable greater buy-in from church members to help cocreate a more transformative faith community.

CONCLUSION

In proposing an abortion abolition framework that is inspired by the other abolition movements, I am not suggesting that to support abortion abolition means that one must support prison abolition or any other abolition struggle. In fact, one need not think a particular institution or practice should eventually be abolished altogether to engage in the methodologies behind abolition. For example, regardless of what one thinks the eventual outcome of prisons should be, one can still engage in the positive imagining project of thinking what a world would look like in which, at the very least, incarceration was very rare and figure out how to create structures to enable that possibility. Similarly, some people on the pro-choice side may say that even in the best of all worlds, there will still be the need for abortion. But they can still engage in the abortion abolition project of creating a world in which, at the very least, there would be relatively little need for abortion.

The pro-life versus pro-choice paradigm has run its course. It enables successful fund-raising for pro-life and pro-choice nonprofit organizations to perpetually organize against their "enemies" on the other side of the divide. It enables politicians to mobilize the constituents of whatever side they represent to advance their political careers. But neither the pro-choice nor the pro-life movement is capable of truly promoting life and freedom for women, their unborn children, and their communities. Rather, we need collective imagining and strategizing among all people to bring a better world into place that honors all. This can happen more easily when we decenter criminalization of abortion as the goal rather than as one possible strategy and then collectively and honestly assess all strategies to see if they are actually accomplishing what they purport to do. While I do not think the criminalization of abortion is an effective strategy given its multitude of negative consequences, I think it would still be easier for those who would agree with me to work with those who disagree on that issue if all opened our eyes to the plethora of strategies we could all engage in.

An abortion abolition framework may seem pie-in-the-sky. Why imagine a world that seems impossible? First, abortion abolition helps us evaluate our strategies to determine if they are taking us closer to or further away from our vision of God's justice and life. We always come up with strategies that seem like good ideas. But if we reevaluate our strategies constantly in light of our vision, we are less likely to keep doing a strategy that does not work or causes unintended harm.

Most importantly, what seems impossible today can be possible tomorrow. As Jesus states: "What is impossible with man is possible with God" (Luke 18:27). Remaining open to insights and direction from God, wherever God may appear, let us build an impossible world together.

CHAPTER 6

Responses from Evangelicals4Justice Board Members

REV. ANDREW CHEUNG

IN THE PRECEDING CHAPTERS, Smith has laid out a compelling argument for "abortion abolition," tracing various social, historical, and theological influences that have informed the two dominant positions toward abortion, either for or against. She signals that neither the pro-life nor the pro-choice position includes a fully coherent response to unwanted pregnancies. Smith has put her finger on one aspect of the conversation that helps us to step outside our narrow outlooks on the issue. I would like to explore further how she fundamentally invites us toward a reimagination of "being" rather than becoming entrenched in moral identity.

Smith states, "[A]n abolition methodology calls for a different approach. It recognizes that the world we want to create is one for which we have no words" (12). In chapter 5, she adds that this "different approach" is primarily "theological because it imagines a world beyond what is given or what can even be described—in short, the kingdom of God" (66). I invite us to consider the conditions in this world where abortion might no longer be necessary. As a follower of Jesus, I believe the kind of world where abortions are abolished is a world where humans become more faithful image-bearers of God toward all of God's creation, especially toward our unborn children and the women who carry them.

This act of reimagining the world begins with changing our questions. We often ask "what," as in: "What is the right position to have?" or "What does the Bible say about the rights of unborn children versus the rights of pregnant women?" or "What are the impacts of a particular law on the rights and freedoms for children, women, and communities?" Instead, asking "who?" brings the starting point back to the kind of people *we ourselves are becoming*. The question of who begins with us rather than with those people "over there." The shared life goal for followers of Jesus is to become more like him in character, word, and deed because we find that in becoming like him, we become the fullest version of ourselves. Christ invites us in Mark 8:35 (NIV) to this type of becoming, "For whoever wants to save their life will lose it, but whoever loses their life for me and for the gospel will save it." These words perhaps hit close to home, particularly in light of the very real loss of life (of children) and livelihood (of women) when it comes to the impacts of abortion and unwanted pregnancies. Yet, each individual must navigate this challenging call of Jesus with Spirit-guided discernment. This process of becoming like Christ isn't merely an individual pursuit.

The "we" in the question invites us to imagine a new degree of "relationality" (using Smith's language) that includes others, not just our own individual moral positions or the shared moral positions of our particular community or sociopolitical affiliation. The "we" is meant to include the communities we easily identify with *and* those with whom we have little or no shared experiences. This "we" approach changes how we interact with those with whom we might disagree. Rather than demonize and publicly shame, at worst, or legislate and sue, at best, the "other side," there is another way of relationality.

Smith shares a wisdom she has learned:

> However, an abolition methodology calls for a different approach. It recognizes that the world we want to create is a world for which we yet have no words. . . . True faith is not grounded in fear and remains open to where Jesus might be sharing a word with us. In that spirit, I offer wisdom I have learned from diverse sources, not to convince people that I have the "right" answer but to open more space for collective thinking on how we can go forward in creating a better world for all. (12–13)

Similarly, an audience member on the late-night comedy show, *The Daily Show*, asked the correspondent Jordan Klepper whether he had seen any of his interviewees at political rallies change their minds because of the facts that Mr. Klepper had presented to them. His answer offers similar insight:

> Changing their mind is hard to do. . . . If you actually want somebody to see something that they haven't seen before and cross that divide into believing something else, they have to acknowledge that they have a sense of uncertainty. You have to acknowledge that you have a sense of uncertainty as well. . . . If you can't relate to them like another human being and say, "I too am uncertain about some of these things," then you will never reach them in asking them, as a human being, to come over to a side of better understanding.[1]

This newly imagined world of being, grounded in the idea of who we are becoming in Christ, changes our approach to responding to issues like abortion. It moves us from a paradigm of competing binaries to a *paradigm of becoming*. The answer to the question of "who we are becoming?" must come from outside of ourselves if we are to find a way through contentious and complex issues. Former Czech president and playwright Vaclav Havel writes, "The present crisis of authority is only one of a thousand consequences of the general crisis of spirituality in the world at present. Humankind, having lost its respect for a higher authority, has inevitably

---

1. Daily Show, "Has Klepper Ever Changed."

lost respect for earthly authority as well. Consequently, people also lose respect for their fellow humans and eventually even for themselves."[2]

Havel's vocabulary of "spirituality" and "authority" suggests one viable and shared source to inform a more inclusive shared imagination. Followers of Jesus recognize that the One who holds all authority in the Universe is also the One who lays down his rights, privileges, and authority for a time so that those who choose to trust him may regain meaningful respect for themselves and one another.

The love of God is the most inclusive force in the history of the world, bringing sinners and saints (often self-proclaimed) into life-giving relationships with the Living God of the Universe through God's son, Jesus. For Christ-followers, the "we" in the "who we are we becoming" question is meant to be an ever-widening circle of "we" that brings the mercy, grace, and hope of God to all, including those who are in need on the margins, and deemed disposable by society. In addition, we find that the ever-widening "we" just might include those with whom we may disagree on social or moral issues. From the creation account of our first parents, Adam and Eve, through God's call on Abraham, eventually revealed through God's covenant people, the Hebrew people, and now passed on to the church of Jesus-followers, God's people are called to share the blessing of their life with God to the world. Jesus followers are invited to imagine how the blessing of life with God might be shared with a world that sees abortion as a necessary and legally entitled option for a limited degree of justice to be defended (i.e., pro-choice) or for abortion to be criminalized in order for a limited degree of life to be defended (i.e., pro-life).

As apprentices of Jesus conform our lives to him, we find ourselves moving naturally from the need to be right and self-righteous (although we rarely call ourselves that) to having the capacity to be truly righteous in all the sense that word conveys in Scripture. The biblical idea of righteousness is not a theological concept to assent to but a practical ideal to live out. Righteousness is about rightly

---

2. Havel, "Introduction to Politics," 14.

relating to all of God's creation—the born and the unborn, women who can get pregnant, and women who cannot—in ways that help all humanity to flourish. The life, death, and resurrection of Jesus show us that this kind of righteous life on earth is not only possible for the incarnate God but a possibility for all who dare to look to him and ask, "Who are we becoming?" As Jesus's apprentices, the life-to-come reaches from the future to this present life, and so leads us toward a world where the abolition of abortion, as Smith has laid out, may become a reality sooner rather than later. This is my daring prayer and hope. May it be ours together.

DR. ROB DALRYMPLE

In 2004, we gave birth to our fifth child. We named him Jason. Unfortunately, at the time of his birth, Jason was only twenty weeks in gestation and had died in the womb a few days earlier. Jason's birth had to be induced. When he came into the world, he was stillborn. It was and remains one of the most challenging moments in our lives. Since then, we have lost multiple other children to "miscarriage" (can someone please come up with a better word?). Knowing the trauma we experienced and its continued impact on our lives, I cannot imagine what it would have been like to add the fear of potentially being prosecuted for child abuse. You see, I have never thought of the idea that the birth of our son might be considered an abortion, which, in some states today, would be illegal. Do some pro-life advocates really expect my wife to continue to carry a dead child in her womb?

In this book, Andrea Smith offers a simple alternative that transcends the "pro-life" versus "pro-choice" binary that dominates American abortion debates. Smith sets forth an approach that is neither pro-life nor pro-choice but offers us an alternative way forward.

Smith contends that both pro-life and pro-choice advocates address the wrong questions. Instead, *Abortion Abolition* presents a new paradigm: what "if we change our goal to promoting healthy, vibrant communities in which all lives are valued, [and] we become open to discussing which strategies (including criminalizing or decriminalizing abortion) will be most effective in achieving this goal"? (11). One of Smith's key proposals is that members of both sides of the debate must learn to consider the factors that lead women to have abortions and begin to think strategically concerning the underlying causes that lead women to have abortions.

This book is a breath of fresh air for someone like myself. For years, I had ranked Francis Beckwith's *Politically Correct Death* on my top ten list. Beckwith masterfully articulates the pro-life position, while at the same time systematically dismantling most all of the pro-choice rejoinders with the wit and candor that only Francis Beckwith can produce. As a result, I have been, and remain, convinced that the pro-life position is the only tenable ethical position. Over the years, however, I have begun to question my pro-life position, particularly concerning its implications for society and public policy. It might be fair to say that I have become a "cautious" pro-life advocate. Although several factors have contributed to my "cautious" stance, I will note two here—both of which are well addressed by Smith's essay.

First, my struggles with the pro-life agenda (not with being pro-life) relate primarily to the societal implications of establishing civil laws banning abortion. In particular, I struggled with the question of criminality.[3] Are we to suppose that a woman who has an abortion should be equated with a murderer? It does not seem right to incarcerate someone for an abortion. Nor does it seem compassionate. This is where Smith's work is brilliant. She argues succinctly, yet with tremendous insight, that criminalization is not the best approach. She contends that criminalization is counterproductive. Smith cites research that indicates that making abortion illegal (which in some instances has included punishing women who have had miscarriages) increases the number of abortions: she notes, "As I have argued throughout this chapter,

---

3. NB: My questioning here has had nothing to do with my wife's and my experience. I never considered, until I began writing this essay, that we may have had an abortion or that what we did might have been illegal. In fact, I do not believe it was an abortion. We simply gave birth to our child.

what is currently distinguishing the pro-life movement is less a commitment to life and more a commitment to criminalization, which promotes death, particularly in poor communities and communities of color" (33). So, if banning abortions and making it a criminal act actually leads to more abortions and potentially risks the well-being of women, perhaps the pro-life agenda is not the right approach.

Second, I struggled with the evangelical ethos. That is, the way the pro-life position has been articulated by many within evangelicalism. My experience, both as a lead pastor and as a professor in evangelical Christian institutions for the past thirty-five years, has been that many pro-life evangelicals, while I believe they are rightly concerned for the unborn child, have failed to demonstrate the same care and concern for the mother.

Smith's work affirmed my "cautious" pro-life position on this point as well. She points out that the research indicates that the church's pro-life advocacy may well be encouraging abortions: "A great number of abortions would not happen in evangelical churches if evangelical women who faced an unwanted pregnancy knew they would still be loved, accepted, and supported if their pregnancy and the circumstances behind it were made public" (89).

Smith's work contends that the pro-choice position is fraught with its own inequities. In particular, its advocacy for a woman's right to choose is systematically discriminatory. That is, the freedom to choose is often applicable only to those women who have access to said choices—which regularly excludes the poor and women of color.

Smith contends that the tendency to simplify the debate to the pro-life versus pro-choice binary is a significant part of the problem. She notes, "Both the pro-life and pro-choice positions are actually more similar than they are different, in that they both fundamentally promote racial, economic, and disability disparity, and neither position is capable of promoting life or choice in our communities" (6).

What, then, does she propose? If criminalizing abortion is not the solution, then for those who maintain the humanity of the zygote/embryo/fetus, what is the solution? She sets for the notion of *abortion abolition*, which Smith defines as "a positive project in which we could create new social systems and systems of care in which no one was disposable" (80).

What does this mean? It means that I can be pro-life and, at the same time, uphold an ethic that both empathizes with women and works to make society a better place in which there are fewer abortions and more resources in place so that everyone might flourish. Sounds a lot like a world that Jesus envisioned. A world that may not truly be realized until the New Jerusalem descends. Yet, a world that we are called to work toward in the present. As Smith asks, "Until we have the world we would like, how can we reduce the harm in the meantime?" (80).

At the end of the day, Smith's work has helped me understand that I can have my cake and eat it, too. I can be a conservative pro-life evangelical and an advocate for women at the same time.

REV. DR. SOONG-CHAN RAH

Many years ago, before Donald Trump had even thought about running for president, long before the appointment of three conservative justices, and even longer before the Dobbs decision, I wrote the following blog post. Sadly, much of what I wrote has come true. The question lingers: what is the best strategy going forward?

> Let me say up front that I am pro-life, which is not a popular position right now. But I believe that the Scripture calls us to advocate for all life. However, I am deeply disappointed in those who are supposedly leading this charge in our common political life. And I am deeply disappointed in those of us who have bought into a miracle strategy that has disappointed us for the last thirty years. So, I offer my take on the miracle strategy

Abortion Abolition

against abortion as offered by the religious right for the last thirty years.

STEP 1:
Find a candidate for president who is pro-life. He must be a pure pro-life candidate who is singularly dedicated to overturning *Roe v. Wade* or at least offer up the rhetoric that he would be dedicated to this task. He must not waver (from now on) in this one quest. We must ignore all other elements of the candidates' policies and ignore numerous unbiblical aspects of his platform.

STEP 2:
Get that candidate to win his party's nomination, even if (see above) you end up supporting unbiblical aspects of the candidates' platform. Eventually we may actually like some of these policies.

STEP 3:
Next, get that candidate to win the national election. Be sure to demonize the opposing party's candidate by any means necessary to get your pro-life candidate elected. One potential side effect: we may end up supporting a campaign financing structure that completely destroys and undermines the democratic process.

STEP 4:
Once that president is in office, wait for a death. Or, more realistically, multiple deaths. We will need at least one, most likely two, Supreme Court justices to die. And it has to be the right Supreme Court justices that die. Not one of the ones we like.

STEP 5:
Bring the right nominee for the Supreme Court. He must be someone who is unequivocally pro-life and committed to overturning *Roe v. Wade*. At the same time, there can be no indication in any of his rulings that he is pro-life because that would derail his candidacy. Pray that he is an activist judge (i.e. willing to change the law of the land from the bench on issues like abortion and health

care) but at the same time a non-activist judge (unwilling to change the law of the land from the bench on issues regarding civil rights).

STEP 6:
Wait for the right court case to come along that makes its way through the entire federal court system in a timely fashion, before the makeup of the court changes. So this time, we're NOT praying for a death, at least not the death of one of our judges. Be sure to elect the right president to a second term so that the court's makeup doesn't change again.

STEP 7:
When the right court case comes along, pray that it is worded and framed in just the right way so that it is able to overturn *Roe v. Wade*. We must also pray that none of the justices have shifted in their thinking or that they may actually want to adjudicate the law rather than make the law. (Thanks a lot Justice Roberts for acting upon your judicial morals rather than politicking from the bench).

STEP 8:
Make sure that Congress will not create any new laws that would undermine the SCOTUS decision. So now we must work in every state to ensure that the right candidates get elected into office, even if that means we continue to tolerate unbiblical values in the government.

Essentially, this approach has been our strategy for the last thirty years. How has it worked so far?[4]

As of Spring 2024, surprisingly, the above strategy through Step 7 has occurred with only Step 8 remaining (a significant step given that we will see an increase in the number of abortions in many states and a galvanizing around the issue of abortion rights). We saw the miracle of *Roe v. Wade* being overturned. But we also saw the problematic aspect of neglecting all other Christian values in order to affirm the one value of opposing abortion. The political

4. Rah, "Miracle Abortion Strategy," paras. 19–28.

victory of asserting the value of unborn life simply by overturning a SCOTUS decision has led to larger scale structural damage such as the Trump presidency, the January 6 insurrection, hateful rhetoric toward those on the margins, and even the disgracing of the evangelical brand in US society. Similar to the Scopes Trial in the early years of the twentieth century, the Dobbs decision of the early years of the twenty-first century may prove to be a pyrrhic victory. We may have won one battle (with limited long-term impact) but lost the larger war for the embodiment of the good news of Jesus. Christian witness may have lost its salt.

Any debate on abortion has become reduced to a purely political battle. Theological nuance and graciousness are no longer a part of the equation. It is now an all-or-nothing, win-at-all-costs strategy. Unfortunately, that strategy's side effects may become more costly to the Gospel in the long run. For those of us who find ourselves in the pro-life camp, but not on board with the miracle SCOTUS strategy, could there have been an alternative narrative or strategy? This book, *Abortion Abolition: Beyond Pro-Life vs. Pro-Choice Politics* seeks to provide just that.

Moving Forward

REV. DR. MAE ELISE CANNON

ONE OF THE MOST profound aspects of Smith's abolition theology is the deconstruction of "sinners" and "saints" in the midst of liberative theology and the oppressed vs. oppressor paradigm. When one considers the teachings of Jesus and Christ's disproportionate concern for the poor and the God whom James Cone identifies as the "God of the Oppressed," it is easy to fall into the false binary of sinners and saints. But Smith helps readers understand the God of creation stands against all oppression, regardless of the perpetrator. As Romans 3:23 reminds readers, "All have sinned and fallen short of the glory of God" regardless of our class, race, culture, or part one plays in society.

As it relates to abortion, the primary goal of minimizing abortions can be achieved pragmatically regardless of one's theological assumptions about the inherent right to life (or not) of the human embryo and whether or not it deserves protection at various stages of its development. For those of us who are ardently pro-life, we must create space to work alongside those who might have common goals, but disagree with our methodology (and/or theological assumptions). I agree wholeheartedly that it is time to reject the pro-choice and pro-life paradigms and the false duality they present. Our goal must be the preservation of life—all life—including that of the mother and especially those in our society who are often marginalized, disregarded, unseen, or ignored. In addition, Smith candidly points out how in both the pro-life and pro-choice movements, often it is women of color who pay the greatest price and the consequences for the criminalization of abortion or exclusion in decision making. Together, as a collective society with diverse theological and ideological perspectives, we must come together and work toward "abortion abolition" while we collectively promote life, freedom for women, their unborn children, and their communities. For those of us who choose to follow Jesus, might we humbly engage, wholeheartedly embracing a strategy that will ardently preserve life, respect the autonomy and choices of women, while also honoring diverse perspectives present in society, and working toward the common goal of abortion abolition.

Moving forward, there must be a third way; a creative alternative to the current reality that moves beyond false binaries and restrictive dualities. So much in the United States today seems to be restricted to the black and white, yes or no, uncompromising dualism that exists in so many areas of American society from our politics and party choices, to progressive or conservative fiscal policies, to right or wrong methodologies. I wish we had the luxury of being so certain all the time!

Rejecting the certitude of political evangelicalism, might we truly follow the Prince of Peace and the one who said, "I am the way and the truth and the life" (John 14:6). Might God grant us grace and peace abundantly, that we might be obedient to that which God uniquely equipped and created each of us individually and collectively to be and to do, through the sanctifying work of the Spirit, into living hope through the resurrection (1 Peter 1:2–3). And in the end, might one of the fruits of that faithfulness be abortion abolition.

Bibliography

"Abortion-Rights Marchers Crowd D.C." *Bridgeport Connecticut Post*, April 26, 2004.
Abraham, Priya. "The Abolitionist." *World* 21 (November 4, 2006) 39–40.
———. "Let My People Go!" *World* 22 (February 24, 2007) 16–19.
Alexander, Michelle. *The New Jim Crow: Mass Incarceration in the Age of Colorblindness*. New York: New, 2010.
Alford, Deann. "Free at Last." *Christianity Today* 51 (March 2007) 30–35.
Anderson, Connie. "Fighting against Human Trafficking on the Abolitionist Plunge." InterVarsity Justice Programs, n.d. http://up.intervarsity.org/content/fighting-against-human-trafficking-abolitionist-plunge.
Ayers, David J. "Current Sexual Practices of Evangelical Teens and Young Adults." Institute for Family Studies, August 2019. https://ifstudies.org/ifs-admin/resources/final-ifsresearchbrief-ayers-evangelicalsandsex8819.pdf.
Balmer, Randall. *Bad Faith: Race and the Rise of the Religious Right*. Grand Rapids: Eerdmans, 2021.
———. "The Real Origins of the Religious Right." *Politico*, May 27, 2014. https://www.politico.com/magazine/story/2014/05/religious-right-real-origins-107133.
Bandarage, Asoka. *Women, Population, and Global Crisis: A Political-Economic Analysis*. London: Zed, 1997.
Beaty, Katelyn. "Portland's Quiet Abolitionist." *Christianity Today* 55 (November 2011) 26–30.
Belser, Ann. "Local Marchers Have Many Issues." *Pittsburgh Post-Gazette*, April 26, 2004, A4.
Beutin, Lyndsey P. "Black Suffering for/from Anti-trafficking Advocacy." *Anti-Trafficking Review* 9 (2017). https://www.antitraffickingreview.org/index.php/atrjournal/article/view/261/245.
Black, Joe. "Marchers Rally for Abortion Rights." *Houston Chronicle*, April 26, 2004, A1.
Blunt, Sheryl Henderson. "The Devil's Yoke." *Christianity Today* 51 (March 2007) 38–39.

Bibliography

———. "The Unflappable Condi Rice." *Christianity Today* 47 (September 2003) 43–48.

Boseley, Sarah. "Criminalising Abortion Does Not Cut Number of Terminations, Says Study." *Guardian*, May 11, 2016. https://www.theguardian.com/world/2016/may/11/criminalising-abortion-does-not-cut-number-of-terminations-says-study.

Box, Steve, and Chris Hale. "Economic Crisis and the Rising Prisoner Population in England and Wales." *Crime and Social Justice* 17 (1982) 20-35.

Briggs, Megan. "Boz Tchividjian to SBC: This Is How Your System Is Broken." ChurchLeaders (blog), October 8, 2019. https://churchleaders.com/news/363528-boz-tchividjian-to-sbc-this-is-how-your-system-is-broken.html.

Brooks, Jonathan. "Race, Gender and Christian Nationalism: The Impact of Trumpism on Evangelicals." Evangelicals 4 Justice and Voices School for Liberation and Transformation Zoom conference, January 30, 2021.

Broom, Fiona. "Abortion Rates Highest Where Legally Restricted: Study." *Sci Dev Net*, July 23, 2020. https://www.scidev.net/global/news/abortion-rates-highest-where-legally-restricted-study/.

Bruce, Billy. "More than Jailhouse Religion." *Charisma* 23 (September 1997) 52–59.

Butterfield, Fox. "Study Shows a Racial Divide in Domestic Violence Cases." *New York Times*, May 18, 2000, A16.

Cadbury, Deborah, dir. *Human Laboratory*. Horizon Series. Documentary film. London: BBC, 1995.

Camosy, Charles. *Beyond the Abortion Wars: A Way Forward for a New Generation*. Grand Rapids: Eerdmans, 2015.

Camplain, Ricky, et al. "Racial/Ethnic Differences in Drug- and Alcohol-Related Arrest Outcomes in a Southwest County from 2009 to 2018." *American Journal of Public Health* 110.S1 (January 1, 2020) S85–S92. https://doi.org/10.2105/AJPH.2019.305409.

"Campus Life: Abortion: Common at Christian Colleges?" *Christianity Today* 33 (July 14, 1989) 42–43.

Cannon, Mae Elise. *Beyond Hashtag Activism: Comprehensive Justice in a Complicated Age*. Downers Grove, IL: InterVarsity, 2020.

———. *Social Justice Handbook: Small Steps for a Better World*. Downers Grove, IL: InterVarsity, 2009.

Care Net. *Study of Women Who Have Had an Abortion and Their Views on Church*. LifeWay Research, November 2015. https://lifewayresearch.com/wp-content/uploads/2015/11/Care-Net-Final-Presentation-Report-Revised.pdf.

Cho, Eugene. Plenary speech, Justice Conference, Chicago, June 6, 2015.

Claiborne, Shane. "A Dialogue on What It Means to Be Pro-Life." *Red Letter Christians*, January 22, 2013. https://www.redletterchristians.org/a-dialogue-on-what-it-means-to-be-pro-life/.

Bibliography

Claiborne, Shane, and Tony Campolo. *Red Letter Revolution: What If Jesus Really Meant What He Said?* Nashville: Thomas Nelson, 2012.

Coleman, Diane. "Face to Face: Challenging the 'Better Dead Than Disabled' Message," Not Dead Yet, September 1, 2016. https://notdeadyet.org/2016/09/face-to-face-challenging-the-better-dead-than-disabled-message.html

Colson, Charles. "God Behind Bars." *Christian Life* 47 (September 1985) 28–32.

———. *Justice That Restores.* Wheaton, IL: Tyndale, 2001.

———. *Life Sentence.* Old Tappan, NJ: Revell, 1979.

———. "Prison Reform: Your Obligation as a Believer." *Christian Life* 41 (April 1980) 23–24, 50–56.

———. "Sentenced for Life." *Moody* 80 (February 1980) 28–70.

———. "Who Will Help Penitents and Penitentiaries?" *Eternity* 28 (May 1977) 12–17, 34.

———. "Why Charles Colson's Heart Is Still in Prison." *Christianity Today* 27 (September 16, 1983) 12–14.

Colvin, Mark. "Controlling the Surplus Population: The Latent Functions of Imprisonment and Welfare in Late U.S. Capitalism." In *The Political Economy of Crime*, edited by B. D. MacLean, 154–65. Scarborough: Prentice-Hall, 1986.

Committee on Women, Population and the Environment, internal correspondence, 1999.

Cone, James. *God of the Oppressed.* Maryknoll, NY: Orbis, 1997.

Consistent Life Network. "Mission Statement." n.d. https://www.consistentlifenetwork.org/mission.

"Controversy over Sterilization Pellet." *Political Environments* 1 (Spring 1994) 9.

Crum, Gary, and Thelma McCormack. *Abortion: Pro-Choice or Pro-Life?* Washington, DC: American University Press, 1992.

Currie, Elliott. *Crime and Punishment in America.* New York: Metropolitan, 1998.

Daily Show, The. "Has Klepper Ever Changed a Trump Supporter's Mind?" Youtube, 4:22, March 20, 2024. https://www.youtube.com/watch?v=t1CoYEMzq8k.

Dart, Bob. "Abortion-Rights Backers March." *Dayton Daily News*, April 26, 2004, A1.

Dart, Bob, and Mary Lou Pickel. "Abortion Rights Supporters March." *Atlanta Journal-Constitution*, April 26, 2004, 1A.

Davis, Angela Y. *Abolition Democracy: Beyond Empire, Prisons, and Torture.* New York: Seven Stories, 2011.

———. *Are Prisons Obsolete?* New York: Seven Stories, 2003.

Dean, Jamie. "Just as I Am." *World* 31 (April 2, 2016) 34–40.

Dellinger, Jolynn, and Stephanie K. Pell. "The Criminalization of Abortion and Surveillance of Women in a Post-Dobbs World." Brookings, April 18, 2024. https://www.brookings.edu/articles/the-criminalization-of-abortion-and-surveillance-of-women-in-a-post-dobbs-world/.

DeRoche, Craig, et al. *Outrageous Justice*. Washington, DC: Prison Fellowship, 2019.

Diemer, Tom. "Thousands Rally for Choice; 500,000 to 800,000 March in D.C in Support of Abortion Rights." *Cleveland Plain Dealer* (April 26, 2004): A1.

Dingle, Shannon. "I Was in the Pro-Life Movement. But Then, Widowed with 6 Kids, I Prepared for an Abortion." *USA Today*, October 12, 2020. https://www.usatoday.com/story/opinion/voices/2020/10/11/abortion-miscarriage-pro-life-choice-widow-column/5909096002/.

"The *Dobbs v. Jackson* Decision, Annotated." *New York Times*, May 7, 2023. https://www.nytimes.com/interactive/2022/06/24/us/politics/supreme-court-dobbs-jackson-analysis-roe-wade.html.

Dobson, Ed, and Cal Thomas. *Blinded by Might: Why the Religious Right Can't Save America*. Grand Rapids: Zondervan, 1999.

Donziger, Steven. *The Real War on Crime*. New York: HarperCollins, 1996.

Downen, Robert, et al. "Abuse of Faith: Investigation Reveals 700 Victims of Southern Baptist Sexual Abuse over 20 Years." *Houston Chronicle*, February 10, 2019. https://www.chron.com/news/investigations/article/Investigation-reveals-700-victims-of-Southern-13591612.php.

Faundes, Anibal, and Iqpal Shah. "Evidence Supporting Broader Access to Safe Legal Abortion." *International Journal of Gynecology and Obstetrics* 131 (2015) S56–S59.

"Fear Not the Disabled." *Christianity Today* 49 (November 2005) 28–29.

Feldt, Gloria. *The War on Choice: The Right-Wing Attack on Women's Rights and How to Fight Back*. New York: Bantam, 2004.

Forbes, Cheryl. "What Hope for America's Prisons." *Christian Herald* 105 (April 1982) 32–40.

Freedman, Alix. "Two Americans Export Chemical Sterilization to the Third World." *Wall Street Journal*, June 18, 1998, A1.

Gadoua, Renee. "A Woman Should Decide." *Syracuse Post-Standard*, April 26, 2004, B1.

Gibson, Gail. "Thousands Rally for Abortion Rights." *Baltimore Sun*, April 26, 2004, 1A.

Gilliard, Dominique DuBois. *Rethinking Incarceration: Advocating for Justice That Restores*. Westmont, IL: InterVarsity, 2018.

Gilmore, Ruth Wilson. "Making Abolition Geography in California's Central Valley with Ruth Wilson Gilmore." *Funambulist* 21 (January-February 2019). https://thefunambulist.net/magazine/21-space-activism/interview-making-abolition-geography-california-central-valley-ruth-wilson-gilmore.

Gold, Rachel Benson. *Lessons from Before Roe: Will Past Be Prologue?* New York: Guttmacher Institute, March 2003.

Gordon, Victor. "Abortion and the New Testament." In *Abortion: A Christian Understanding and Response*, edited by James Hoffmeier, 73–85. Grand Rapids: Baker, 1987.

Bibliography

Gorman, Michael J. "The Use and Abuse of the Bible in the Abortion Debate." In *Life and Learning V: Proceedings of the Fifth University Faculty for Life Conference, June 1995, at Marquette University*, edited by Joseph W. Koterski, SJ, 140–76. Washington, DC: University Faculty for Life, 1996.

Graham, Ruth. "Southern Baptists Grapple with Racist History." *Al Jazeera America*, April 1, 2015. http://america.aljazeera.com/articles/2015/4/1/in-wake-of-ferguson-southern-baptists-grapple-with-racist-history.html.

Griffith, Lee. *The Fall of the Prison: Biblical Perspectives on Prison Abolition*. Grand Rapids: Eerdmans, 1993.

Guttmacher Institute. "Unintended Pregnancy and Abortion Worldwide." Guttmacher Institute, July 2020. https://www.guttmacher.org/fact-sheet/induced-abortion-worldwide.

Hackett, Erna Kim. "Why I Stopped Talking about Racial Reconciliation and Started Talking about White Supremacy." *Feisty Thoughts*, August 23, 2017. http://feistythoughts.com/2017/08/23/why-i-stopped-talking-about-racial-reconciliation-and-started-talking-about-white-supremacy/.

Harper, Lisa Sharon. "We Go There: Abortion." *Red Letter Christians*, August 27, 2020. https://www.redletterchristians.org/we-go-there-abortion/.

Hart, Drew G. I. *Who Will Be a Witness? Igniting Activism for God's Justice, Love, and Deliverance*. Harrisonburg, VA: Herald, 2020.

Hartmann, Betsy. *Reproductive Rights and Wrongs: The Global Politics of Population Control*. Boston: South End, 1995.

Harvey, Bob. "Christians and Crime." *Faith Today* 18 (September/October 2000) 30–36.

Havel, Vaclav. "An Introduction to Politics, Morality and Civility." In *Summer Meditations*, by Vaclav Havel, 14. New York: Knopf Doubleday, 1991.

Heggen, Carolyn Holderread. *Sexual Abuse in Christian Homes and Churches*. Scottdale, PA: Herald, 1993.

"Historical Abortion Law Timeline: 1850 to Today." Planned Parenthood, n.d. https://www.plannedparenthoodaction.org/issues/abortion/abortion-central-history-reproductive-health-care-america/historical-abortion-law-timeline-1850-today.

Hoffmeier, James. "Abortion and the Old Testament Law." In *Abortion: A Christian Understanding and Response*, edited by James K. Hoffmeier, 49–64. Grand Rapids: Baker, 1987.

Ignatieff, Michael. *A Just Measure of Pain: The Penitentiary in the Industrial Revolution, 1750–1850*. New York: Pantheon, 1978.

Inman, Shasta N. "Racial Disparities in Criminal Justice: How Lawyers Can Help." American Bar Association, September 18, 2020. https://www.americanbar.org/groups/young_lawyers/publications/after-the-bar/public-service/racial-disparities-criminal-justice-how-lawyers-can-help/.

Jankovic, Ivan. "Labour Market and Imprisonment." *Crime and Social Justice* 8 (1977) 17–31.

Jenkins, Jack. "In Dallas, Southern Baptist Leaders Gather to Address Church Abuse." *Religious News Services*, October 4, 2019. https://religionnews.

com/2019/10/04/in-dallas-southern-baptist-leaders-gather-to-address-church-abuse/.

Jewell, Dawn Herzog. "Red Light Rescue." *Christianity Today* 51 (January 2007) 28–37.

Jones, Robert P. Lecture at "Race, Gender and Christian Nationalism: The Impact of Trumpism on Evangelicals" conference. Evangelicals 4 Justice, January 30, 2020.

Jones, Robert P., Daniel Cox, and Rachel Laser. "Committed to Availability, Conflicted about Morality: What the Millennial Generation Tells Us about the Future of the Abortion Debate and the Cultural Wars." Public Religion Research Institute, Inc., June 6, 2011. https://www.prri.org/research/committed-to-availability-conflicted-about-morality-what-the-millennial-generation-tells-us-about-the-future-of-the-abortion-debate-and-the-culture-wars/.

Jordan, A. "Toxicology of Depot Medroxyprogesterone Acetate." *Contraception* 49.3 (1994) 189–201. doi: 10.1016/0010-7824(94)90037-x.

Justice Fellowship. *Jubilee Extra* 1–6 (February 2000) 1–3.

Justice, Jessilyn. "Setting the Sex-Trafficked Captives Free." *Charisma* 41 (June 2016) 38–46.

Kessler, Glenn. "Planned Parenthood's False State: 'Thousands' of Women Died Every Year before Roe." *Washington Post*, March 29, 2019.

Kim, Mimi E. "The Carceral Creep: Gender-Based Violence, Race, and the Expansion of the Punitive State, 1973–1983." *Social Problems* 67.2 (2020) 251–69.

Kovach, Bill. "Final Approval of Abortion Bill Voted in Albany." *The New York Times*, April 11, 1970. https://www.nytimes.com/1970/04/11/archives/final-approval-of-abortion-bill-voted-in-albany-rockefeller-to-sign.html.

Krust, Lin, and Charon Assetoyer. *A Study of the Use of Depo-Provera and Norplant by the Indian Health Services.* Native American Women's Health Education Resource Center. Lake Andes, SD: 1993.

Lakota People's Law Project. "Native Lives Matter." Lakota People's Law Project, February 2015. https://lakota-prod.s3-us-west-2.amazonaws.com/uploads/Native-Lives-Matter-PDF.pdf.

Lawton, Kim. "So What Should We Do with Prisoners?" *Christianity Today* 32 (November 4, 1988) 38–39.

Lee, Morgan. "Life after Prison." *Christianity Today* 60 (September 2016) 38–47.

Leslie, Christopher. "Antitrust Amnesty, Game Theory, and Cartel Stability." *Journal of Corporation Law* 31 (2006) 453–88.

———. "Trust, Distrust, and Antitrust." *Texas Law Review* 82 (February 2004) 515–680.

Lewis, Andrew R. *The Rights Turn in Conservative Christian Politics: How Abortion Transformed the Culture Wars.* Cambridge: Cambridge University Press, 2018.

Losen, Daniel J., et al. "Suspended Education in California." The Civil Rights Project, April 10, 2012. http://civilrightsproject.ucla.edu/resources/

projects/center-for-civil-rights-remedies/school-to-prison-folder/summary-reports/suspended-education-in-california.

Lyons, Scott Richard. *X-Marks: Native Signatures of Assent*. Minneapolis: University of Minnesota Press, 2010.

MacKinnon, Amy. "What Actually Happens When a Country Bans Abortion." *Foreign Policy*, May 16, 2019. https://foreignpolicy.com/2019/05/16/what-actually-happens-when-a-country-bans-abortion-romania-alabama/.

Madigan, Erin. "Hundreds of Thousands March for Abortion Rights." *Milwaukee Journal Sentinel*, April 26, 2004, 3A.

Maher, Lisa. "Criminalizing Pregnancy—The Downside of a Kinder, Gentler Nation?" *Social Justice* 17 (Fall 1990) 115–35.

Mancini, Michael. *One Dies, One Gets Another*. Columbia: University of South Carolina Press, 1991.

"Marchers Say Bush Policies Harm Women." *Marin Independent Journal*, April 26, 2004.

Marinucci, Carla. "Hundreds of Thousands in D.C. Pledge to Take Fight to Polls." *San Francisco Chronicle*, April 26, 2004, A1.

Masterson, Mike, and Patricia Gutherie. "Taking the Shot." *Arizona Republic*, 1986.

Metzger, Paul Louis. *Connecting Christ: How to Discuss Jesus in a World of Diverse Paths*. Nashville: Nelson, 2012.

Mill, Manny. "No Prisons in Heaven." *New Man* 8 (January/February 1999) 74.

Millet, Lydia. "Native Lives Matter, Too." *New York Times*, October 13, 2015. https://www.nytimes.com/2015/10/13/opinion/native-lives-matter-too.html?emc=eta1&_r=1.

Mink, Gwendolyn, ed. *Whose Welfare?* Ithaca: Cornell University Press, 1999.

Morgante, Camden. "5 Purity Culture Myths and Why They Are False Promises." *Christians for Biblical Equality*, May 28, 2019. https://www.cbeinternational.org/resource/article/mutuality-blog-magazine/5-purity-culture-myths-and-why-they-are-false-promises.

Mulvihill, Geoff, and Kimberlee Kruesi. "Which States Could Have Abortion on the Ballot in 2024?" *AP News*, April 10, 2024. https://apnews.com/article/abortion-ballot-amendment-ban-protection-states-2024-052ff9846f8416efb725240af22b92ec.

National Advocates for Pregnant Women. "What's Wrong with Making It a Crime to Be Pregnant and to Have a Drug Problem?" National Advocates for Pregnant Women, March 9, 2006. https://www.nationaladvocatesforpregnantwomen.org/whats_wrong_with_making_it_a_crime_to_be_pregnant_and_to_have_a_drug_problem/.

National Law Center on Homelessness and Poverty. "Housing Not Handcuffs 2019: Ending the Criminalization of Homelessness in U.S. Cities." Washington, DC, December 2019. http://nlchp.org/wp-content/uploads/2019/12/HOUSING-NOT-HANDCUFFS-2019-FINAL.pdf.

Nelson, Jennifer. *Women of Color and the Reproductive Rights Movement*. New York: New York University Press, 2003.

Bibliography

Nolan, Pat. "Justice e-Report: Study Shows 'Neighborliness' Reduces Crime." *Justice Fellowship* (email newsletter), 2004.

———. "Two New Laws Provide Important Justice Reform." *Justice Fellowship* (email newsletter), 2004.

Norsigian, Judy. "Quinacrine Update." *Political Environments* 3 (Spring 1996) 26–27.

Olasky, Marvin. "The Life of a Slave." *World* 25 (February 13, 2010) 25–27.

———. "Pro-Life Priorities." *World* 15 (January 15, 2000) 34.

O'Rourke, Lawrence. "Thousands Rally for Abortion Rights." *Minneapolis Star Tribune*, April 26, 2004, 1A.

Paltrow, Lynn, and Jeanne Flavin. "Arrests of and Forced Interventions on Pregnant Women in the United States, 1973–2005: Implications for Women's Legal Status and Public Health." *Journal of Health Politics, Policy and Law* 38 (April 2013) 299–343.

Panetta, Grace. "The States Passing Strict Abortion Bans Have Some of the Highest Maternal and Infant Mortality Rates in the Country." *Business Insider*, June 1, 2019. https://www.businessinsider.com/states-passing-abortion-bans-have-highest-infant-mortality-rates-2019-5.

Patchesky, Rosalind. *Abortion and Women's Choice: The State, Sexuality, and Reproductive Freedom*. Rev. ed. Boston: Northeastern University Press, 1990.

Phelps, Timothy. "Demonstration in D.C." *New York Newsday*, April 26, 2004, A05.

Piper, John. "Is It Sinful to Be Pregnant before Marriage?" Ask Pastor John, December 14, 2016. https://www.desiringgod.org/interviews/is-it-sinful-to-be-pregnant-before-marriage.

———. "Policies, Persons, and Paths to Ruin: Pondering the Implications of the 2020 Election." Desiring God, October 22, 2020. https://www.desiringgod.org/articles/policies-persons-and-paths-to-ruin.

Powell, Charles. "America's Ugliest Crime." *Charisma* 35 (November 2009) 40–41.

Price, Clive. "The Day Slavery Ended." *Charisma* 32 (February 2007) 40–44.

Prison Fellowship. "1997 Criminal Justice Crime Index." Prison Fellowship, 1998. https://www.prisonfellowship.org/.

———. "Prison Fellowship's Statement on Communities of Color." Prison Fellowship, November 2020. https://www.prisonfellowship.org/2020/11/prison-fellowships-statement-on-communities-of-color/.

Prison Fellowship International. *Portraits of Reconciliation*. Washington, DC: Prison Fellowship International, 1988.

Pulliam, Russ. "A Better Idea than Prison." *Christian Herald* 110 (November 1987) 28–31.

Rah, Soong-Chan. "A Miracle Abortion Strategy that Has Accomplished What?" Prof. Rah's Blog, October 31, 2012. https://profrah.wordpress.com/videos/.

Bibliography

———. "Soong-Chan Rah Says Black Lives Matter Because of What Experienced." National Black Evangelical Association, November 28, 2015. Used with permission.

Rainwater, Lee. *And the Poor Get Children: Sex, Contraception, and Family Planning in the Working Class.* Chicago: Quadrangle, 1960.

Reed, Ralph. *Active Faith: How Christians Are Changing the Soul of American Politics.* New York: Free, 1996.

Richie, Beth E. *Arrested Justice: Black Women, Violence, and America's Prison Nation.* New York: NYU Press, 2012.

Riskind, Jonathan. "Supporters of Abortion Rights Seek Forefront." *Columbus (OH) Dispatch*, April 25, 2004, 1A.

Roberts, Dorothy. *Killing the Black Body: Race, Reproduction, and the Meaning of Liberty.* New York: Pantheon, 1997.

Robinson, Haddon. "CT Readers Survey: Sex, Marriage, and Divorce." *Christianity Today* 36.15 (December 14, 1992) 29–31.

Rosenthal, Elisabeth. "Legal or Not, Abortion Rates Compare." *New York Times*, October 12, 2007. https://www.nytimes.com/2007/10/12/world/12abortion.html.

Ross, Loretta, and Lynn Roberts. *Radical Reproductive Justice: Foundation, Theory, Practice, Critique.* New York: Feminist Press at CUNY, 2017.

Ruggiero, Vincenzo. "An Abolitionist View of Restorative Justice." *International Journal of Law, Crime and Justice* 39.2 (2011) 100–110.

Ryan, Joseph. "Abortion Rights Supporters Jump In to Rejuvenate Cause." *Chicago Daily Herald*, April 26, 2004, 15.

Saheli Collective. *Quinacrine: The Sordid Story of Chemical Sterilisations of Women.* New Delhi, India: July 1997.

Saletan, William. *Bearing Right: How Conservatives Won the Abortion War.* Berkeley: University of California Press, 2004.

———. "Electoral Politics and Abortion: Narrowing the Message." In *Abortion Wars: A Half Century of Struggle, 1950–2000*, edited by Rickie Solinger, 111–23. Berkeley: University of California Press, 1998.

Salvatierra, Alexia, and Peter Heltzel. *Faith-Rooted Organizing: Mobilizing the Church in Service to the World.* Downers Grove, IL: IVP, 2014.

Saxton, Martha. "Disability Rights." In *The Abortion Ward*, edited by Rickie Solinger, 374–93. Berkeley: University of California Press, 1998.

Scimone, Diana. "Stop Child Slavery Now." *Charisma* 35 (November 2009) 34–38.

Segars, Melissa. "Rally for Women's Rights." *Madison (WI) Capital Times*, April 26, 2004, 1A.

Sherman, Lawrence W., and Heather M. Harris. "Increased Death Rates of Domestic Violence Victims from Arresting vs. Warning Suspects in the Milwaukee Domestic Violence Experiment (MilDVE)." *Journal of Experimental Criminology* 11 (March 2015) 1–20. https://doi.org/10.1007/s11292-014-9203-x.

BIBLIOGRAPHY

Sider, Ron. "Why I'm Voting for Hillary Clinton." *Christianity Today* 60 (October 2016) 54–56.

Silliman, Jael, and Ynestra King, eds. *Dangerous Intersections: Feminist Perspectives on Population, Environment, and Development.* Boston: South End, 1999.

Silliman, Jael, et al. *Undivided Rights: Women of Color Organize for Reproductive Justice.* Cambridge, MA: South End, 2004.

Simmons-Duffy, Selena, and Elissa Nadworny. "6 Key Facts about Abortion Laws and the 2024 Election." *NPR*, May 22, 2004. https://www.npr.org/sections/health-shots/2024/05/22/1252771024/state-abortion-laws-2024-election.

Smarto, Don, ed. *Setting the Captives Free! Relevant Ideas in Criminal Justice and Prison Ministry.* Grand Rapids: Baker, 1993.

Smietana, Bob. "Mega Shepherd." *Christianity Today* 48 (February 2004) 28–35.

Smith, Andrea. "Better Dead Than Pregnant: The Colonization of Native Women's Reproductive Health." In *Policing the National Body: Race, Gender, and Criminalization*, edited by Jael Silliman and Anannya Bhattacharjee, 123–46. Cambridge, MA: South End, 2002.

———. "Beyond Pro-Choice versus Pro-Life: Women of Color and Reproductive Justice." *NWSA Journal* 17.1 (2005) 119–40. http://www.jstor.org/stable/4317105.

———. *Conquest: Sexual Violence and American Indian Genocide.* Cambridge, MA: South End, 2005.

———. "Evangelicals and Abolitionist Methodologies." *Religions* 13.9 (2022) 1–12. https://doi.org/10.3390/rel13090811.

———. "The Moral Limits of the Law." *Settler Colonial Studies* 2.2 (2012) 69–88.

———. *Native Americans and the Christian Right: The Gendered Politics of Unlikely Alliances.* Durham: Duke University Press, 2008.

———. *Unreconciled: From Racial Reconciliation to Racial Justice in Christian Evangelicalism.* Durham: Duke University Press, 2019.

Smith, Tammie. "Marchers Call for 'a Choice' about Reproductive Rights." *Richmond (VA) Times Dispatch*, April 26, 2004, A1.

Solinger, Rickie. *Beggars and Choosers: How the Politics of Choice Shapes Adoption, Abortion, and Welfare in the United States.* New York: Hill & Wang, 2001.

State Congress of North Carolina. "House Bill 1430, Norplant Requirement/Funds. General Assembly of North Carolina." May 17, 1993.

Stephenson, Kathy. "Utahns Take Part in D.C. and at Home." *Salt Lake Tribune*, April 26, 2004, A6.

Stock, Jacquelin L., et al. "Adolescent Pregnancy and Sexual Risk-Taking among Sexually Abused Girls." *Family Planning Perspectives* 29 (1997) 200–203, 227.

Sweeney, Annie. "Chicagoans Head to D.C. for Pro-Choice March." *Chicago Sun-Times*, April 25, 2004, 18.

Toner, Robin. "Abortion Rights Marches Vow to Fight Another Bush Term." *New York Times*, April 26, 2004, A1.
"Tracking the Rise of U.S. Slave Traffic." *Reject Apathy* 1 (2011) 8.
Van Ness, Daniel. "The Crisis of Crowded Prisons." *Eternity* 36 (April 1985) 33–37.
———. "Restoring Crime's Victims." *Eternity* 38 (1987) 8–14.
Varoqua, Eman. "N.J. Supporters Form Large Column for Rights." *Bergen County (NJ) Record*, April 26, 2004, A01.
Vogelstein, Rachel B., and Rebecca Turkington. "Abortion Law: Global Comparisons." Council on Foreign Relations, October 28, 2019. https://www.cfr.org/article/abortion-law-global-comparisons.
Walker, Samuel. *Sense and Nonsense about Crime*. Belmont: Wadsworth, 1998.
Walker-Barnes, Chanequa. *I Bring the Voices of My People: A Womanist Vision for Racial Reconciliation*. Grand Rapids: Eerdmans, 2019.
Walsh, Mary Williams. "Abortion Horror Stories Spur Inquiry: Canada; Questions Raised after Women Allege Hospital Denied Them Anesthesia as Punishment." *Los Angeles Times*, April 3, 1992, A5.
Whitehead, John. "Death Control." *Rutherford* 4 (1995) 11.
Winner, Lauren. *Real Sex: The Naked Truth about Chastity*. Grand Rapids: Brazos, 2006.
Wolfe, Elizabeth. "Rights March Packs Mall." *Memphis Commercial Appeal*, April 26, 2004, A4.
Wynn, Kelli. "Hundreds Go to D.C. for March Today." *Dayton Daily News*, April 25, 2004, B1.
Yong, Amos. *The Bible, Disability, and the Church: A New Vision of the People of God*. Grand Rapids: Eerdmans, 2011.

www.ingramcontent.com/pod-product-compliance
Lightning Source LLC
Chambersburg PA
CBHW031347160426
43196CB00007B/757